Then & Now

John Peters
David Couling Michael Ridley

Elizabeth Caroline Peters (nee Leigh) (1884-1960). This book is dedicated to the memory of my mother, who always recalled her young days in Victorian and Edwardian Bournemouth with great affection and who always thought of others before herself.

Published 1978

Published by
Blandford Press Ltd.,
Link House, West Street,
Poole, Dorset, BH15 1LL.
ISBN 0 7137 08719
Printed and bound in Great Britain by
Biddles of Guildford Ltd.

Contents

Introduction

Bournemouth lies on the great heath between the ancient towns of Christchurch and Poole. 170 years ago it would have been hard to imagine the famous seaside resort situated on this site.

A visit to Bourne Bottom at Branksome will give the reader a clear picture of the heathland interlaced with paths. The golf links of Queens Park and Meyrick Park also show how beautifully wild it must have been. A few fishermen's turf hovels and the home of wild game was all that it could boast. In the 18th century it was a popular haunt for smugglers who were referred to as "Gentlemen of the Night".

The name of Bournemouth is older than many think. In preparing a report of the area in 1574 the Earl of Southampton referred to it as an easy landing place for invaders to our shores.

Two names of distinct local interest appear on a map dating from the first half of the 17th century. One is Alum Chine Copperas House and the other Boscombe Copperas House, where in the latter part of the 16th century James Blunt, 6th Lord of Mountjoy of Canford, opened "Mynes". He was the first man in Europe to successfully extract alum from shale in the manufacture of copperas for tanning, ink making and other kindred purposes. Due to litigation and lack of finance, these industries failed. What became of the local "mynes" is a matter for conjecture.

In 1796 with Europe under Napoleon, and Britain in danger of invasion, a troop of Dorset Yeomanry under Captain Lewis Tregonwell was ordered to patrol the 7 miles of coastland called Poole Bay, which the town of Bournemouth faces. Tregonwell's other duties were to support the Revenue Officers in enforcing the law against smugglers, the majority of whom were murdering scoundrels, ably assisted by the local inhabitants, who were pleased to receive the contraband.

Tregonwell has been called "The Founder of Bournemouth". He was certainly the first to foresee its potential as a resort, for whilst staying with his rich wife at Mudeford in 1810, he visited the mouth of the Bourne again, whereupon they decided to purchase some land upon which to build a house.

Between 1816 and 1822 he purchased more land, being encouraged by the renting out of his original mansion, and the marine village of Bourne started to grow. Advertisements for cottages he built appeared at frequent intervals in the *Salisbury and Wiltshire Journal.* Here then was the genesis of the modern holiday industry.

The ground work for this development had already been done in 1802, when Sir George Tapps, the Lord of the Manor of Westover, and some of his neighbours agreed between themselves it would be an advantage to the district if the communal rights were changed to absolute ownership. To this end they procured the passage of the necessary Act of Parliament known as the Christchurch Enclosure Act, 1802.

Despite Sir George Tapp's development east of the Bourne, under the guidance of the famous architect Benjamin Ferrey, the population in 1851 was only 695. Ferrey's ambitious scheme envisaged a planned fashionable resort. The Westover Villas, some dozen buildings which lined the north side of Westover Road, even until the 1920's, were a fine example of his work.

Much of Bournemouth is still as it was in Victorian and Edwardian times. The fact that many of the houses and premises are still in use is not only a tribute to the builders of those days, but to the planners of the town, of whom Mr. Christopher Crabbe Creeke, subsequently the town's first surveyor, is but one.

It may be of interest to recount, that in the accounts of the Overseers of the Poor in Holdenhurst Church Chest, there is an entry in 1743 for £1 4s. 0d for the repairing of Bourne Plank, and again in 1763 a record of one Joseph Trokes Bill doing similar work at Bourne Plank for £1 3s. 1d. These accounts are the first known references to a bridge over the riverlet, the Bourne Stream, and the names of the men who repaired it over 200 years ago. The bridge over the Square was still called Holdenhurst Bridge in 1856 and the valley of the Bourne was known as Holdenhurst Bottom.

A statement made before the Magistrates in 1774 by a Will Harris, a seafaring man, shows he was born at a place called Decoy Pond, in the Parish of Holdenhurst, which place can justifiably be called "the Mother of Bournemouth". There was, in fact, a Decoy Pond for wild ducks, measuring about 135 feet x 66 feet, some 300 yards from the present Square, near the war memorial. A dwelling house of some description is known to have existed in 1762, where Debenhams store is today. The present Coy Pond more than a mile further up the valley was formed sometime in the 1880's when the railway embankment was made.

An extract from Leigh's Road Book of England and Wales of 1831 is of interest, as reference to Bournemouth were rare in those days. *"Bourne Cliffe or Tregonwell's Bourne, about 6 miles from Christchurch on the road to Poole is a modern built watering place. The sands are extensive and several bathing machines are kept. There is an Inn".* The "Inn" referred to was the Tapps Arms, built by Sir George Tapps in 1809, which was ostensibly kept for fishermen's accommodation and picnic parties but derived its main income from the smugglers and their kindred business. It was the only place of rest and refreshment for travellers between Christchurch and Poole, on the barren heath that is now modern Bournemouth.

Even in 1884, it was recorded that it was possible for a man to walk on a late summer evening at twilight from the Turnpike Gate in Poole, to the top of Christchurch High Street through Bournemouth without meeting a soul the whole way!

The advent of the railway extension into the Town in the 1870's brought Bournemouth within economic reach of many visitors from far afield and gave considerable impetus to its growth, which within a few years, was phenomenal. From a population in 1871 of 6,507 it rose by 1881 to 16,859 and by 1900 to nearly 60,000! Its present population is over 150,000.

In 1857 there were 14 hotels and 38 lodging houses, the comparable figures today are astronomic by comparison. Bournemouth owes much to the planning and foresight of its founders, for making a town of grace and dignity, that is not only attractive to those fortunate enough to live here, but also to the vast numbers of holiday seekers.

With varied exceptions the scope of this book is limited to the administrative boundary of the Borough of Bournemouth. As an interesting discourse of what Bournemouth was like during Victorian and Edwardian times we have included extracts from contemporary guide books which help add life to the photographs.

Discovering Ancient Bournemouth

This picture, taken about 1922, shows workmen unearthing a Bronze Age burial (see inverted urn at right of picture) at Hengistbury Head.

There is a popular myth that Bournemouth has little or no history. The town, of course, only dates from the Victorian era but long before this it was inhabited by men, who readily appreciated its many attractions as a place to live.

The name is not new. It is mentioned in Saxton's map of Dorsetshire of 1575 and it is recorded that men from Bournemouth took part in the defence of the South from the Spanish Armada in 1588.

The earliest known remains of man in the Borough were found at Longham in September, 1932, when water engineers unearthed a Neolithic skull, now known as the 'Bournemouth Man'. Thought to be over 5,500 years old, it was one of the few Neolithic skulls recovered in the south of England. It was examined by Sir Arthur Keith, the famous anatomist, and later John Cameron included a chapter on it in his 'Skeleton of British Neolithic Man' published in 1934. Unfortunately the skull was alone and had probably been deposited in its resting place seven feet below the surface of the ground by the force of a stream long since disappeared.

Although the skull is the earliest actual remains of man that has been found in Bournemouth, well over 3,000 Palaeolithic flint implements dating from about 300,000 B.C. have been discovered in the 100 foot gravel terraces. Many of these were discovered during the construction of the railway line at Boscombe and Pokesdown. Others have been found at Southbourne, Moordown and Talbot Woods, and very fine specimens from Wentworth Avenue, Boscombe and Wootton Mount, Lansdowne.

The earliest settlement in Bournemouth is to be found on Warren Hill, Hengistbury Head. Commonly called the 'Reindeer Hunter' camp, it dates to the Upper Palaeolithic period, about 10,000 B.C. The use of the term 'reindeer hunters' is unfortunate, as these people also hunted the horse, and neither horses nor reindeer bones have been found on the site.

Hengistbury Head is one of the richest and most important archaeological sites in the Borough; indeed, in the country. People interested in pre-history all over the world know of it. Apart from the Upper Palaeolithic sites, numerous Mesolithic (Middle Stone Age) flint implements have been found, both inside and outside the Double Dykes (Iron Age fortification).

Excavations on Hengistbury Head, conducted by J. P. Bushe Fox in 1911-12 uncovered not only important evidence of Iron Age occupation on the site but also a burial of an important person of the Wessex culture of the early Bronze Age, whose grave contained his gold-covered cloak buttons, a necklace of amber beads and a bronze halberd amulet. A fine gold bracelet of the Romano-British period was also found during the 1911-12 excavations. Certainly the most important and prolific period of occupation of Hengistbury Head was the Iron Age and Romano-British period. The great earthen bank and ditch fortifications known as the Double Dykes were erected during this period. Inside the Dykes there grew up an important settlement. Excavations revealed not only hut circles but numerous coins of a new type, and smelting areas where they had been made. These coins known as 'Hengistbury class', have been found at other sites on Wessex. Excavations on the Dykes, however, did not reveal any evidence of a palisade fortification, nor of any battle in defence of the settlement, which might have been expected from the Roman invasion.

Left: A Bronze Age double-looped palstave. One of the numerous archaeological discoveries made in Bournemouth during the town's development.

Below: The skull of the Bournemouth Man, in reality a woman! Thought to be over 5,500 years old, it was found near Longham in September 1932. It is one of the few Neolithic skulls found in the South of England.

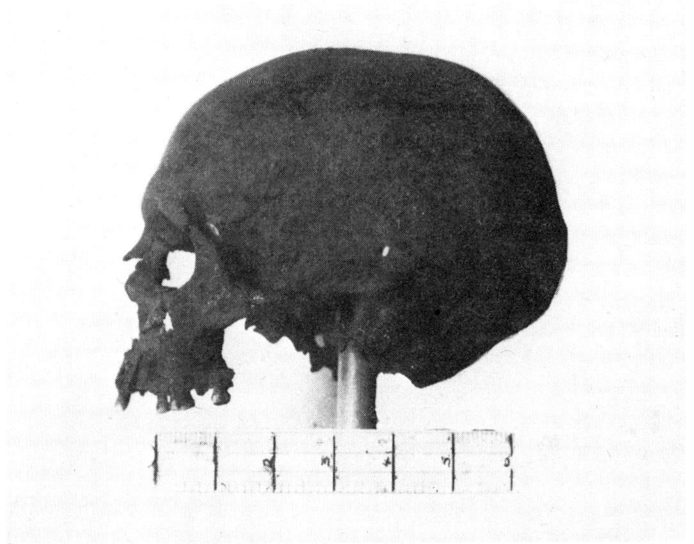

The people of Hengistbury belonged to the Durotrigian tribe, and Hengistbury seems to have been an important town, if not an area capital. The interesting fact to note is that, unlike Maiden Castle, near Dorchester, which has yielded ample evidence of Roman attack, Hengistbury has not. All the evidence points to a long and continuous association with the Romans before, during and after their invasion. This is unusual but a parallel can be found in the Chichester area, ruled by the great Roman-Briton, Cogidubnus. Excavations on Hengistbury revealed no burnt huts, no hurried burials, but a continuous sequence of Roman pottery, dating from the first century B.C. to the New Forest pottery of the Roman-British period. Hengistbury coins were minted after the Roman invasion and were found alongside the Roman coins. The people, then, seem to have been little troubled by the Romans, who allowed them to retain their own way of life. They were tolerent of, even friendly with, Rome trading with them, the Romans on their part, by-passing them on condition that they remained friendly. Recent discoveries of a Roman fort on St. Catherine's Hill, which overlooks Hengistbury Head and the river ways into Wessex, indicate that the Romans, however, thought it advisable to retain a small garrison in the area to keep an eye on them.

Hengistbury, however, cannot claim all the limelight, for Bournemouth, is perhaps one of the richest archaeological areas in Britian. It was popular with the Beaker folk of the early Bronze Age. Beakers have been recovered from Talbot Woods, others have been found at Boscombe, Kinson and Sheepwash.

During the Bronze Age, Bournemouth seems to have been extremely popular with a group of farmers known as the 'Deverel-Rimbury' people. Originally from Europe they crossed the English Channel to settle at various places including East Anglia, Sussex, Wessex, Cornwall - and especially in Bournemouth. Cemeteries have been found at Wick, Kinson, Moordown and

Pokesdown; and burials at Iford and the Lansdowne etc. A cremation cemetery was also found at Latch Farm near Christchurch. With well over 400 burials, the total number of cremations from Bournemouth is the highest anywhere in the country. Bournemouth's only Neolithic long barrow was excavated at Holdenhurst by Stuart Piggott in 1936.

Apart from the Bronze Age burials, important bronze finds of the Bronze Age have been made in Bournemouth. Palstaves (axes) have been found at Irving Road and Belle Vue Road, Southbourne and at Pokesdown where a spear head was also found. A spear-head was also recovered from Wick. Talbot Woods and Littledown Avenue, Queens Park have yielded palstaves with a very rare Iberian type being found in the middle of the road near Five Ways, Charminster in 1894. A Sicilian type of the shaft-hole axe was fished up off Southbourne in 1937 and an early Bronze Age flanged axe was found by a schoolboy on Hengistbury Head in 1953. Socketed axes have been found at Hengistbury Head, Tuckton and Southbourne.

Numerous artifacts such as Neolithic polished axes flint scrapers, Bronze Age flint arrow-heads etc. have been found all over Bournemouth including Winton, Redhill, Charminster Road, Boscombe, Westbourne, Tuckton, Iford, Castle Lane, Lansdowne, Moordown, Kinson etc.

The Iron Age is well represented in Bournemouth. Apart from the settlement at Hengistbury Head, occupational evidence has been found at Strouden Park and Ensbury Park; at Lascelles Road, Leigh Vale Road, Hillbrow Road and Droxford Road, Pokesdown; at the Grove, Lawford Road, and Headswell Crescent Redhill Common; at Burleigh Road and Foxholes Road, Southbourne; at Dukes Coppice, Russel Road and Weyman's Avenue, Kinson and at Tuckton and Iford.

The settlement at Strouden Farm which was discovered in 1929 produced not only Iron Age pottery but also Romano British New Forest ware and a fragment of Roman Samian pottery, probably of the Antonine period. The Ensbury Park site was discovered by workmen in 1935 and produced Iron Age pottery as well as clay loom weights and burnt daub from hut walls with impressions of wattle and finger prints.

The most important Iron Age discovery was not made until 1969, when the reconstruction of the Overcliff Drive on the East Cliff revealed an extensive Iron Age settlement. The excavations that followed revealed numerous banks and ditches, and a vast quantity of Iron Age pottery, spanning a period of approximately two hundred years, being abandoned in the 3rd century A.D. The site extended Eastwards from the Carlton Hotel to what is today the Riviera Flats.

With recent rebuilding programmes many new finds are being made and interested field workers are still making finds on the well known sites such as Hengistbury Head which has produced a unique Iron Age iron adze, a stone ritual object (probably foreign in origin) coins, numerous flint tools and pottery. In 1976 a unique Gallo-Belgic Gold stater, circa 80 B.C. was found at Hengistbury Head on the harbour foreshore. Finds have also been made at Kinson, Moordown, Kings Park etc. and at Holdenhurst where a large Sarsen megalith, weighing over one and a half tons was discovered during the construction of the new Bournemouth Ringwood Road. It was probably brought there by Neolithic man from the Marlborough Downs and may be connected with the Holdenhurst long barrow.

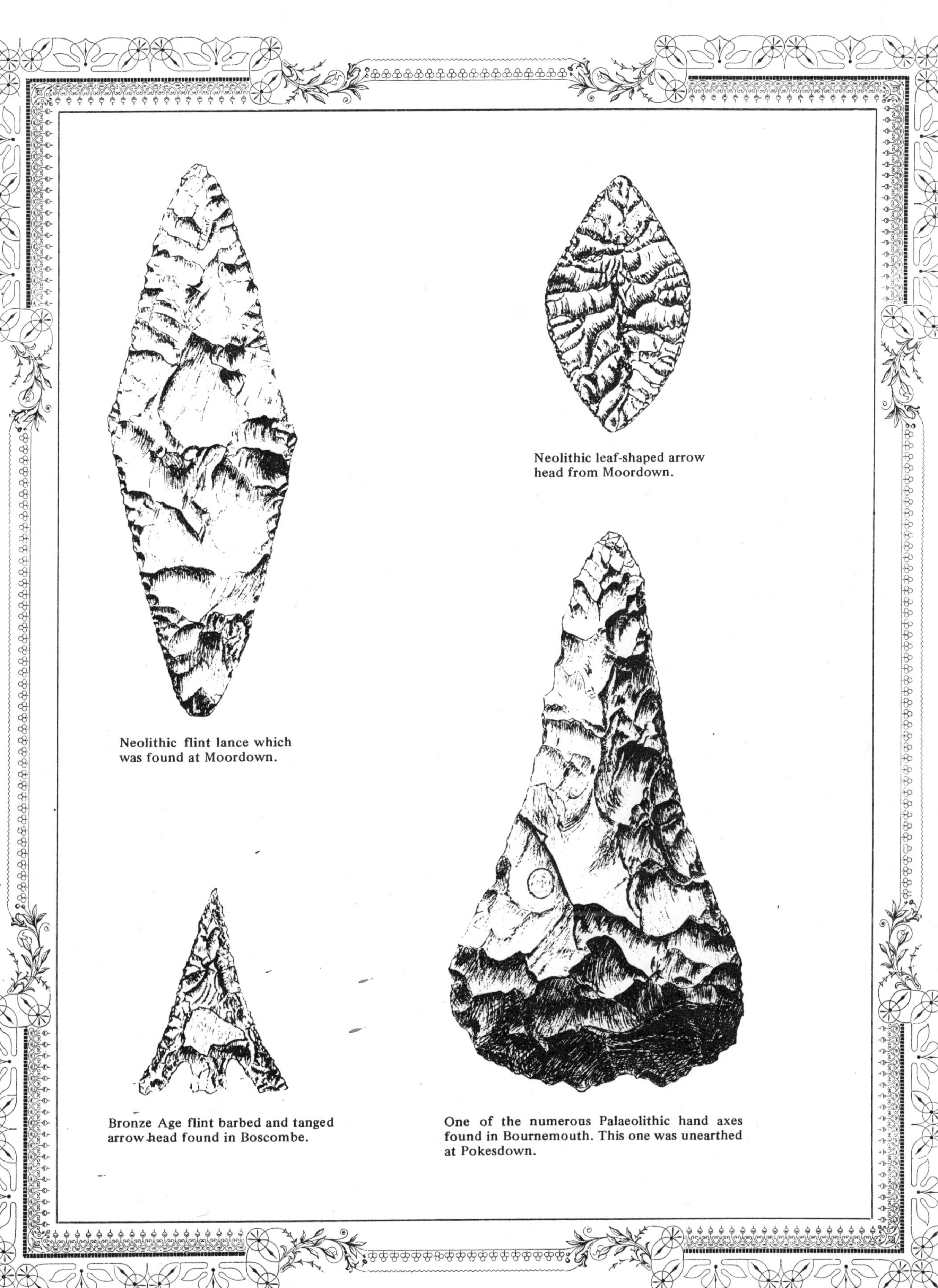

Neolithic leaf-shaped arrow head from Moordown.

Neolithic flint lance which was found at Moordown.

Bronze Age flint barbed and tanged arrow head found in Boscombe.

One of the numerous Palaeolithic hand axes found in Bournemouth. This one was unearthed at Pokesdown.

The photographer, Robert Day in his studio.

Early Photographers

It is almost certain that the art of photography arose from the desire of the painter to find an accurate way in which to reproduce images. Indeed, Louis Daguerre (1787-1851) was himself a notable French artist, who no doubt dreamed of creating his dioramas without the bother of painting the huge surfaces. The first permanent pictures were made by Daguerre in 1839; his process gave one picture, a positive on a plate of silvered copper, for each exposure. Daguerre was also the first to discover the latent image. He had attempted to secure a visible image on the plate by exposure in the camera, with little success. By accident Daguerre found that by exposing the plate in the camera for a short time, then exposing it to the vapour of mercury, a complete image formed and became visible.

In England, Henry Fox-Talbot was working on the same problem, and in 1841 discovered the process of making negative images on paper. The negatives represented the light parts of the subject as black or opaque and the dark parts as white or transparent. By placing this negative on a fresh piece of sensitive paper and exposing it to light a positive print was obtained. It was from this process, rather than from Daguerre's, that photography has developed. It was left to the English sculptor, Frederick Scott Archer (1813-1857), to invent the wet collodion plate. These collodion plates were coated in a solution of silver nitrate and were exposed and developed while the plates were still wet.

Robert Day (1822-73), Bournemouth's first photographer, almost certainly experienced the difficulty of using the wet plate process. It is more than likely that Day had to employ a porter to convey his equipment around, whilst he recorded the development of Bournemouth in it's early days. Day's porter would have had to manhandle, probably in a hand-cart, one or two plate cameras, a large wooden tripod, several lenses, bottles of chemicals, glass plates, dishes, scales and weights, measures and funnels, and fresh water if none was at hand, plus a dark-room tent. I doubt whether photography would be quite so popular today, if that's what it entailed to take a photograph of Aunt Maud sitting on the sands of Bournemouth.

The amateur has also played his part in the development of photography. Richard L. Maddox (1816-1902) was an English doctor and amateur photographer, who in 1871 invented the dry plate, a glass plate coated on one side with a film of gelatine, that was much easier to use than the wet plate. This invention, which did not come into widespread use until 1880, coupled with that of Professor Herman W. Vogel (1834-1898), who produced the first ready-made dry plates for sale, allowed the amateur to try his hand in the art of photography. But this did not please the professionals, Vogel was heard to say in his defence "not everybody who got hold of a violin is as yet a violinist and not everybody who got hold of a dry plate is as yet a photographer".

In the 1890's, the first true amateur's camera came on to the market, the Kodak roll film camera, made by George Eastman. This simple camera measuring 105mm x 88mm x 88mm (6½'' x 3½'' x 3½'') incorporated a sensitive emulsion paper roll, which took one hundred circular 63mm (2½") pictures.

The great appeal of Eastman's Kodak camera was that the camera with the film inside had to be returned to the factory for developing and printing. The camera was then sent back, with 100 mounted prints and a new film loaded ready for use. Eastman's slogan was "You press the button, we do the rest". Indeed, by the 1900's, the "button" was being pressed by millions. The Eastman Kodak Company, gave the amateur photographer what Henry Ford gave the man in the street, availability, reliability, and cheapness.

In 1927 Eastman received the Progress Medal of the Royal Photographic Society of Great Britain, for his great strides in photography. George Eastman died in 1932, taking his own life ("My work is done - why wait?"), we owe much to the man, and his work.

St. Andrew's Presbyterian Church photographed in 1872 by Robert Day, whose photographic hut is on the right by the Church. Bournemouth's first photographer, he is responsible for many of the photographs in this book.

PHOTOGRAPHIC APPARATUS.

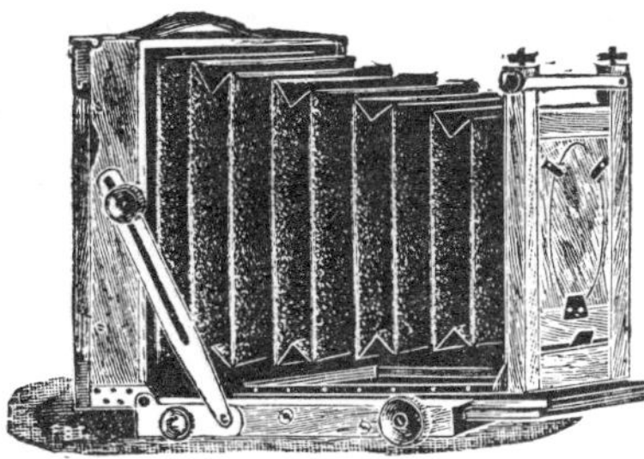

ALL OF THE

PRINCIPAL MAKERS' GOODS

IN STOCK.

FREE LESSONS.

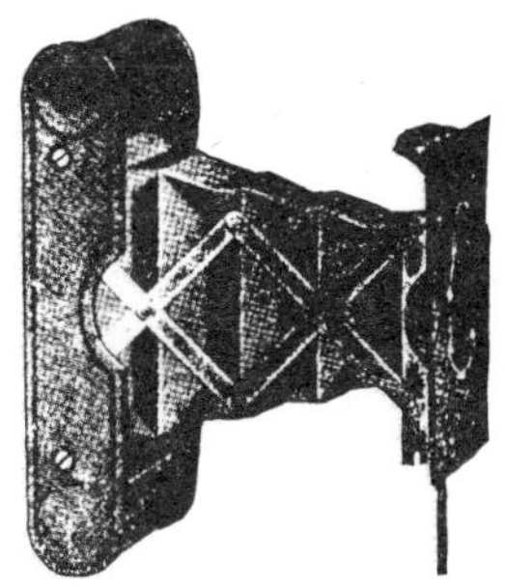

HAND CAMERAS - - - - from 12s. 6d. to £16 16s. 0d.
STAND CAMERAS - - - - - ,, 12s. 9d. to £25 0s. 0d.

Lenses, Tripods, Shutters, Plates, etc., etc.

NEW AND SECOND-HAND

Cameras and all Apparatus taken in Exchange.

All Photographic Appliances on Hire . . .
. . . Use of Dark Room free to Amateurs.

ARTISTIC PHOTOGRAPHY.

MIELL & RIDLEY,

Art Photographers and Portrait Painters,

3, VICTORIA BUILDINGS,

Old Christchurch Road,

BOURNEMOUTH.

Studio & Reception Rooms on Ground Floor.

OUTDOOR PHOTOGRAPHY
AND
LARGE GROUPS A SPECIALITY.

The Largest & most Complete Series of Photographs of Bournemouth Scenery.

ROBERT DAY,

PHOTOGRAPHER,

BOURNEMOUTH

(Studio, near the Scotch Church.)

R. D. begs to thank the Inhabitants and Visitors of Bournemouth for the liberal patronage he has received during the last five years, and hopes by strict attention, combined with cleanness and sharpness in his prints, using only the best chemicals, and availing himself of the most recent discoveries, to retain a share of their patronage.

PRICES.

Cartes de Visite.		Card Vignette.	
One Copy	2*s.* 6*d.*	One Copy	3*s.*
Six Copies	6*s.*	Six Copies	7*s.*
Twelve Copies ...	10*s.*	Twelve Copies ...	12*s.*
The new Cabinet Portraits.		**Diamond Cameo Portraits.**	
One Copy	3*s.*	One Copy	3*s.*
Six Copies	12*s.*	Six Copies	8*s.*
Twelve Copies ...	21*s.*	Twelve Copies ...	15*s.*

If more than one figure in the picture, 1s. for each additional sitter will be charged.

Two negatives are taken when a dozen copies are required.

Miniature Portraits for Lockets, Brooches, &c., executed in the first style of art, on Opal, Glass, Paper, Mica, &c., at equally low prices.

Half-plate Vignettes from five shillings to twenty-one shillings. Enlargements, if required, in the first style of finish.

Negatives, when approved of, kept, and copies can always be had.

R. D. is prepared to execute Photographs of Views and Residences of the neighbourhood at very moderate charges, and respectfully solicits an inspection of his recent productions.

R. D.'s Views of Bournemouth and its vicinity, from Carte de Visite size up to 12 inches by 10, may be obtained at SYDENHAMS' LIBRARY, and at TRIBBETT AND MATE's Directory Office.

N. B.—Ladies' and Children's Portraits are taken by Miss DAY, if preferred.

With photography becoming accessible to the amateur, the world became a mass of pictures. The proud owner of a Box Brownie could, and did snap everything, both moving and still. A fatal fascination of the time, was the family dog. He was snapped for posterity in every possible attitude. Sitting, standing, dying for his country, jumping, and laying demurely in his owner's arms. The shutter speeds in the Kodak Brownies were rather slow, and this accounts for the rather upsetting attitude of the dog, when taken jumping in the air. He often took on the appearance of a half crazed wolf, leaping at an unseen victim, the pictures being a complete blurr with only a mass of fur and fangs showing. I can recall one dog, by the name of Fraser, who took an instant dislike to having his picture taken. It is known that during his long life, Fraser savaged three Box Brownies and ripped the bellows out of a plate camera.

In 1900, the average family would most certainly have had a box camera, and no outing would have been complete without it. A trip to the beach at Bournemouth would have commenced with a snap of the family outside their home, buckets and spades at the ready. Into the car or coach, another snap before they go off and then to the beach. While travelling, a senior member of the group would take a picture from the moving vehicle, the result being not all that one expected. On the beach father could run riot with his camera, baby paddling at the waters edge, mother sleeping in the deck chair, the building of the sandcastle by the older children, all were scenes to be recorded. No doubt the last snap of the day would be the setting sun playing on the sparkling waters.

Many pictures taken in those days were of a member of the family taking a picture, which of course showed the camera they were using. A valuable record of the types of cameras used in days past. Without the trip to the seaside or country, the snaps in the garden, a vital part of our social history would have been lost forever. For however good the professional photographer was, he trod a different path. It was left to the amateur to show us life in the raw, in the early days of photography.

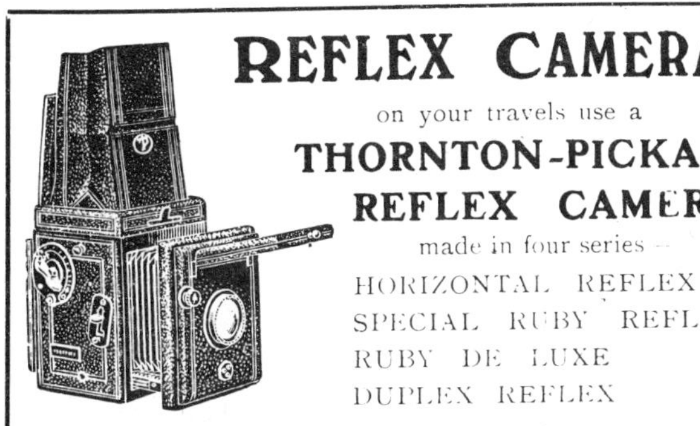

One amateur may very much differ from another in respect of the degree to which he cultivates his hobby. There are people who expose only a few rolls of film per year, while others regularly devote a great deal of time to photography and so become experts of the art. One of many was Mrs. Julia Margaret Cameron, who took up photography on the Isle of Wight in 1863, when she was 48. Cameron knew many famous people and made many of them sit for her. Her work, both in print and negative form has today become very collectable in both England and the U.S.A. But Mrs. Cameron was somewhat of an exception, the majority of amateurs did not attain that degree of ambition and their work has ended its days in drawers, chests and garden sheds.

Apart from the amateur contributions, it is to four professional Bournemouth photographers, Robert Day, the Spinney brothers and Martin Ridley, that we owe a debt, for without their work this book would not have been possible. Day's studio appears in many photographs of The Square, next to the Scotch Church at the bottom of Richmond Hill. His son, W. J. Day, carried on his father's business, then situated in the Lansdowne, Holdenhurst Road area, until 1920. The Bournemouth Municipal Library purchased their photographic collection from Day's son when the business ended. It is now on permanent exhibition in the Library.

William Spinney (1860-1933) owned Blacklock's the chemist in The Square, and with his brother Henry (1882-1962) contributed greatly to recording Bournemouth in the early 20th century. Although both were amateurs, their approach to photography was highly professional. Much of their photographic work was taken up with recording places of interest in and around Bournemouth. They produced a fine set of photographs showing the Bournemouth Centenary Fêtes 1910, considered by many Bournemouth historians to be of great interest in showing the Edwardians' love of the ceremonial. Many of the photographs taken by the brothers were sold in their shop, and Mr. A. M. Lea, nephew to the Spinneys, well remembers being brought into their shop as a young child and seeing the revolving stand displaying their work.

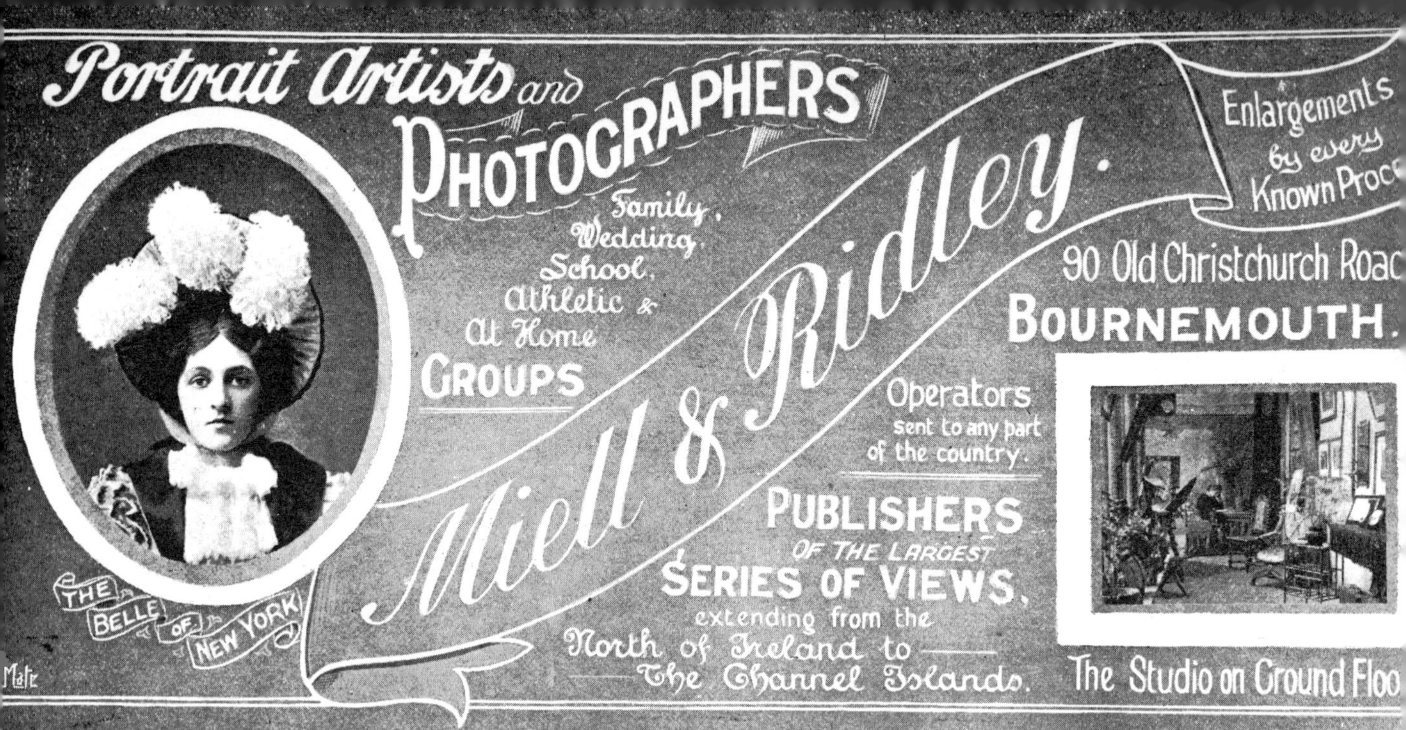

It will be of interest to botanists to know that Frank Spinney, father of William and Henry, was an accomplished botanist himself. Frank Spinney was instrumental in helping Professor Darwin with his investigations into insectivorous plants. Investigations centred around Bournemouth Poor Common, now Meyrick Park, for specimens of the sundew, which then grew in great profusion in the boggy land. William and Henry's father has one other claim to fame; that of being a friend of Robert Louis Stevenson. The Bournemouth Evening Echo relates, "Mr. Spinney cherished among other recollections reminiscences of Robert Louis Stevenson, and his dim inglorious battlefield of the bed and the physic bottle. During his three years residence at Westbourne, Stevenson when able to do so attended service at St. Peter's Church. But he could not escape trouble; even there he again and again had attacts of haemorrhage. On such occasions he would leave the church, saunter up to Messrs. Blacklocks' and place himself under Mr. Spinney's ministrations till his friends arrived from church to accompany him home".

Little is known of Martin Ridley, except that he started work probably just before the First World War, and joined in partnership with Harry Miell, a portrait photographer. Their studio was in Old Christchurch Road. Ridley's speciality was viewcards, and he travelled the whole of the British Isles recording scenes of interest. On his death, Ridley's daughter took over the collection, but due to moving to a new house, Miss Ridley had to abandon it. The collection consisted of several thousand glass plates, and a vast amount of viewcards. The Evening Echo of May 28th, 1964, states, "waste paper merchants may take the postcards, many of which surely would be of value to future historians and collectors. Some may find use for the hundreds of glass plate negatives. But there is still a problem of disposal. It seems a pity that so much will have to be destroyed".

The collection was indeed split; only a few plates stayed in the Town, bought by collectors and the Bournemouth Municipal Library. The greater part of the collection left the town for ever. It is interesting to note that the whole of the collection could, at that time, have been bought for just £5.00. It is a sad reflection on Bournemouth, that the Local Authority could not have, perhaps, purchased the collection, and in doing so kept a valuable visual record of the town intact.

Gone now are the days when one could set up a plate camera in The Square, without the fear of being run over; and of the days, when to see a photographer with his head underneath a dark-cloth, focusing his camera, was an event for young and old alike. Now we are the servants of time, with fast film, motor driven cameras and high speed developers. Perhaps we should give a thought to the photographers of those halcyon days, when time was unimportant and only the composition of the picture and the final result mattered.

The founder of Bournemouth, Louis Dymoke Grosvenor Tregonwell (1758-1832). Captain of the Dorset Yeomanry, he had responsibility for coastal defences during the war with France from 1796 until 1802. Part of his house, which he took possession of on the 24th April 1812, now forms part of the Royal Exeter Hotel. His remains, together with other members of his family, lie in a tomb in St. Peter's churchyard.

Birth of the Town

It is now nearly thirty years since the scenery and capabilities of this retreat were first appreciated by L. D. G. Tregonwell, Esq., of Edmondesham, Dorset, who possessed a considerable portion of the barren heath land, which prevailed everwhere in the immediate neighbourhood. Delighted with the sheltered situation, the genial temperature, that prevailed here at all seasons, the magnificent seaward prospect, and the tranquil retirement that might here be successfully sought, he erected a mansion which became his favourite residence, surrounded with shrubberies and plantations. He also built an inn by the side of the road, then little frequented, and a few cottages, which were occasionally resorted to in the bathing season by invalids desirous of availing themselves of the advantages offered by the natural peculiarities of the spot.

It was reserved however, for Sir George W. Tapps Gervis, Bart. of Hinton Admiral, near Christchurch, to give an efficient impetus to the improvements of which the place was capable. About three years since, being the principal landowner of the neighbourhood, he became satisfied that Bournemouth was endowed by nature with those especial features and circumstances which eminently fitted it to become an approved resort of those who, at the termination of the London season, seek on the coast that envigorating repose, and that commixture of fashion and retirement, which afford the best protection against ennui, and are most conducive to the restoration of that freshness and activity, both in the physical and mental function which the constant excitements of town life have so great a tendancy to undermine. Under his auspices, therefore, and directed by the acknowledged talent and personal superintendance of Mr. B. Ferrey, the eminent architect, many plans for the improvement of the estate were laid down and some of them immediately released. Thus on spots where, before, the foot of man rarely pressed, but the lowly heath flower blossomed and faded in unnoticed solitude, where no sound was heard but the rustling of the rank grass and the wild shrub, as they waved in the light sea breeze - there a number of detached villas, each marked by distinct and peculiar architectural features, have sprung into existence, affording accommodation of varying extent, so as to be suited to the convenience of either large or small families, and adapted, some for extended, others for confined establishments. To all these are attached ample gardens, whilst in the front are shrubberies tastefully laid out and walks arranged with due regard to convenience and effect. At one end of this range stands a spacious and commodious hotel erected for the accommodation of more temporary visitants, and fitted up in the most complete style. All these edifices command views of the ocean, of the distant coast, and of the vale lying immediately beneath, whilst the site is, at the same time, so judiciously chosen, that they are effectually sheltered from the biting winds of the north and east.

First Bournemouth Guide, 1840.

In the "Hampshire Advertiser" of June 16th, 1838, appeared a statement that "the new romantic watering place called Bourne is progressing at a railway pace. The splendid hotel is all but completed, and in a few short years it is conjectured that it will complete with the renown of Southampton". A week later there was an announcement of a prospective sale by auction of "marine villas". The auctioneer was Mr. George Cranston, and the sale was to take place at the Bath Hotel.

As far back as 1826, we find in the "Salisbury and Winchester Journal" an announcement of two "modern detached houses" to let, with the following allurements: "A bathing machine and a warm bath. A baker attends four days a week. A coach passes daily from Southampton to Weymouth, and several carriers".

In 1839 a mansion was advertised at eight guineas a week. It was described as "the property of a lady, and suitable for a family of distinction". It was sheltered by plantations, and "a kitchen garden and two cows" might be rented. Other attractions included three bathing machines, with "a guide" in attendance. Applications were to be made to Mr. George Fox or Miss Toomer; "if by a letter, post-paid"! No doubt the Mansion referred to was that of Mrs. Tregonwell.

Bournemouth 1810-1910.

Painting entitled "Smugglers at Bourne Mouth" by Henry Perlee Parker, which once hung in the Tregonwell Arms. The central figure may be Isaac Gulliver, smuggler extraordinaire. Born in 1745, he was independent of all the villains and rabble who haunted the shores and district. By all accounts, he was a remarkable man. By the very nature of his trade, few facts about him are known, legends nevertheless abound, many of which may be true. His home in Bournemouth was East Howe Lodge, demolished in recent years. He was a man of great daring with a genius for organisation. The loyality of his fifty-strong gang was bound by his fair dealing as an employer. A stern disciplinarian, he forbade violence. As a smuggler, he accumulated wealth and influence. His trade spread from the Solent to Bridport. After obtaining a "King's Pardon", he retired to Wimborne where he died in 1822 at the age of 77. He is buried in the Minster.

Tregonwell's Mansion in 1812. In 1822 he moved into a new residence on the site of the present Hotel Merville. The Marchioness of Exeter leased his original home and in this way Exeter Road got its name.

The Mansion of Louis Tregonwell as it looked in 1883. It still retains in this photograph its original façade which can be recognised today in the Royal Exeter Hotel.

Terrace Cottage in 1870. Originally the home of Tregonwell's gardener, it was re-built to become his family residence. The site is now occupied by the Hotel Merville. Part of the cottage can still be seen in the façade of the Hotel.

Portman Cottage in 1870. Originally built for Louis Tregonwell's butler, Symes, but used as a family residence and for letting purposes. It stood at the junction of Exeter Road and Exeter Park Road.

The Tapps Arms was so named after the Lord of the Manor of Westover, Sir George Tapps. Built in 1809, in what is now known as Post Office Road, it was the first substantial building in Bournemouth. It was rebuilt by Louis Tregonwell in 1812 and renamed the Tregonwell Arms, standing on the site until 1885. It was, at one time, a rendezvous for smugglers. In 1839 the inn was appointed a receiving office for letters by Mr. George Fox, the first Postmaster. Before it was demolished in 1885, it spent its last years as a coffee house under the auspices of the Blue Ribbon Tavern Company.

One of the earliest lithographs of Bournemouth dating about 1836/7 showing Benjamin Ferrey's proposed development for Sir George Tapps. Had the plans been carried out, Bournemouth would present a very different picture today.

Benjamin Ferrey's ambitious plan for the additional development of the "new" Belle Vue Hotel site (now the Pavilion). The Westover Villas and the Bath Hotel with a view across Poole Bay made an attractive picture in 1840.

Ferrey's "plans" for the Gervis Estate in 1840 shows the Westover Villas (1837) and the Bath Hotel (1838). The pier shown did not come into existence until later.

The National Sanatorium in 1860 viewed from Bealesons, which is today Avenue Road. The Sanatorium was built in 1855.

The same view as above, as it appears today.

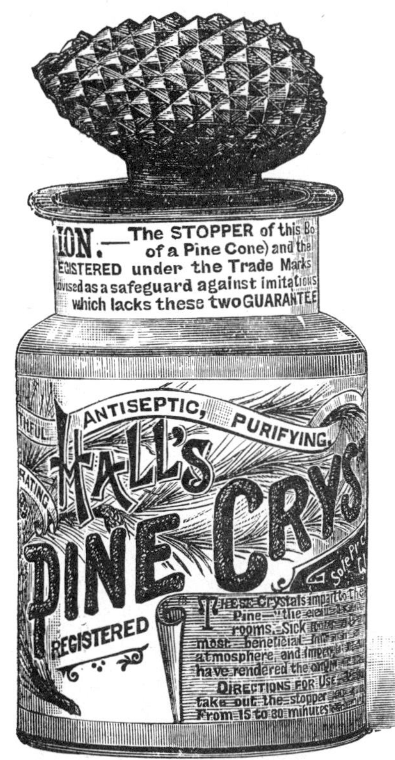

*Prepared from the famous **Bournemouth Pines.***

Hall's Pine Crystals.

*See [that our [**Registered Pine Cone Stopper** is in every Bottle.*

These Crystals impart to the atmosphere the peculiar healthful odour of the Pine Woods, "the cleanest, sweetest and most healing of all Scents." In Bedrooms, Sickrooms, Sitting-rooms, &c., they exert a most beneficial and soothing influence, acting as a pleasant Deodoriser, purifying the Air, and impregnating it with the refreshing sanitary properties which have rendered the neighbourhood of Bournemouth so famous. A most delightful and invigorating Smelllng Bottle.

In JARS, 1/-, 1/6, 2/6, and 3/6 each (Postage 3d.)

A remarkable photograph taken about 1870 of the Upper Gardens; the National Sanatorium is on the left. The villa where the present Town Hall stands was called "The Glen". It was occupied by Rev. E. Wanklyn who subsequently became the first vicar of St. Michael's Church.

The Square in 1863. The building on the left is Victoria Villa, the home of Mr. T. J. Hankinson, the estate agent, whose business was adjacent.

Looking across the lower Gardens towards Victoria Villa and shops. Both the photographs on this page are by Robert Day.

Richmond Hill from The Square in 1873. The Wiltshire and Dorset Bank is on the left and St. Andrew's Presbyterian Church is opposite. The premises of Wiltshire and Dorset's Bank have been taken over by T. J. Hankinson for his estate agency.

The Square in 1875. At the foot of Richmond Hill is St. Andrew's Presbyterian Church and beside it, the wooden shack studio of Robert Day, the photographer.

The view across the Square up Exeter Road in 1865. Today Debenhams, Fortes, Rebbeck's occupy the buildings at the right, though much altered.

Lainston Villa in 1905, in use as the "Garden Tea House", which continued to trade until the late 1920's. The site is now occupied by the Bus Station entrance in Exeter Road facing the Square. Lainston Villa was the home of Mr. Crabbe Creeke, the town's first surveyor. It was used by the local Commissioners from 1857-75.

Left: The view in 1865 by Exeter Road towards Terrace Cottage. The cottage, built in 1815 by Tregonwell, was used as a family residence. The site is now occupied by the Merville Hotel.

Looking down towards the Square from Richmond Hill in 1880. A milkman on his horse and cart makes his way up the hill.

The forerunner of the pier. This engraving shows the wooden jetty of 1855 Bournemouth's first landing stage. Built by public subscription, it consisted of a retractable platform on piles. It was replaced in 1859 by the first pier, which was opened in 1861.

A view of the pier in 1868. On the left is the Belle Vue Hotel, and occupying the present position of the Corporation's Baths is Sydenham's baths.

A view of the pier from the East Cliff in 1872.

A view in 1865 of Brookside and the beach near pier approach. It was a popular place for visitors and residents to relax, enjoying the invigorating air.

Left: A fine example of Mr. Robert Day's photographic art; The Bath Hotel in 1860. Built in 1838, it was later purchased by Merton Russell-Cotes and much enlarged. Under his ownership, it became famous for the quality of its accommodation and cuisine. It was much frequented by royalty.

Right: A view of the Bath Hotel in 1850. The coaches standing outside belong to the private horse bus service, which operated to Christchurch at a cost of half a guinea per seat. The ride took forty minutes.

Below: The Royal Bath Hotel as it is today, one of Bournemouth's top hotels. The original façade can clearly be seen.

BOURNEMOUTH.

The MEDICAL and other AUTHORITIES unanimously recognise and recommend BOURNEMOUTH as possessing the MILDEST CLIMATE in WINTER, the COOLEST IN SUMMER, and the SAFEST BATHING GROUND IN EUROPE.

ROYAL BATH HOTEL

"HOTEL DE LUXE OF THE SOUTH."

Patronised by H.R.H. The Prince of Wales, H.I.M. The Empress Eugenie, H.R.H. The Duchess of Albany, H.M. The King of the Belgians, H.R.H. Prince Albrecht of Prussia, Regent of Brunswick the late Earl Beaconsfield, and many other Royal and distinguished personages.

Selected for the RECEPTION, BALL, and BANQUET by the BRITISH MEDICAL ASSOCIATION, 29th and 30th July, 1891.

Foundation Stone laid on Coronation Day, 1838. Enlarged 1878 and 1888. Electric Light throughout Hotel.

Note.—Rooms Reserved for and Conveyance sent to meet Visitors on receipt of Letter or Telegram.

1,000 Feet Sea Frontage, overlooking the Pier. Grounds Five Acres, Sheltered by Pine Woods, Due South.

SPECIAL NOTE.—THE ONLY HOTEL ON THE EAST CLIFF.

Tariff sent on Application.

he late MR. EDMUND YATES, on his last sojourn here (14th November, 1892), wrote in the Visitors' Book—***"A Charming Hotel, excellently conducted perfect in Comfort, Cleanliness, and Cookery."***

FOR POSITION OF HOTEL SEE PANORAMIC VIEW OPPOSITE.

Looking towards the beach from the pier in 1870.

Passing the time of day. A view of the wooden pier in 1861.

The entrance to the pier c. 1870. This pier, which was replaced by the first iron structure in 1880, was opened by Sir George Meyrick on the 17th September 1873.

Bournemouth Pier in 1872. The SS Heather Bell is seen here leaving the pier for Swanage. The first regular steamship service started on May 1st 1871.

In 1862 Adelaide Villas occupied the western corner of Old Christchurch Road and Yelverton Road.

Granville Cottages in 1862. They stood on the east corner of Old Christchurch Road and Yelverton Road, and were named after Dr. A. B. Granville, whose book "The Spas of England", published in 1941, helped to build up Bournemouth's reputation as a health resort.

The scene in 1863 at Cliff Cottage, built on the West Cliff in 1810. The site now occupied by the Regent Palace Hotel. Charles Darwin stayed here in 1862. Already famous for his book "The Origin of Species", his experiments with the Sundew plant were associated with Mr. F. Spinney, of Blacklock the Chemist.

Left: The sites of Granville Cottages, (Barclay's Bank) and Adelaide Villas (Midland Bank), today one of the busiest parts of Bournemouth.

Right: The Regent Palace Hotel, the site of Cliff Cottage.

Top: Lansdowne Crescent in 1870. There was little built beyond this point. The horse trough and drinking fountain date from 1867.

Left: The drinking fountain and horse trough built in 1867 in Lansdowne Crescent provided a welcome, refreshing drink for tired horses and men after the long pull up the road.

Below: The Lansdowne in 1870 from Bath Road (then New Christchurch Road). Lansdowne House was built in 1868, and from 1891 until it was destroyed by bombing in 1943 the site was occupied by the Hotel Metropole.

The Blacksmith's Forge, which stood for many years at the present entrance to Pokesdown Station, taken in 1880 when its work was vital to the farming community.

The 1870 view of the Pier Approach area, showing the Belle Vue Hotel (now occupied by the Pavilion) and Sydenham's Baths at the peak period. Today in the summer, something like 60,000 vehicles pass this spot every 24 hours. The line of the original Westover Villas in Westover Road can clearly be seen.

Few today will believe this was the view in 1863 from the present Gervis Place entrance of the Bournemouth Arcade. Ashley Cottages at the far end occupied the site of what is now the Criterion Hotel.

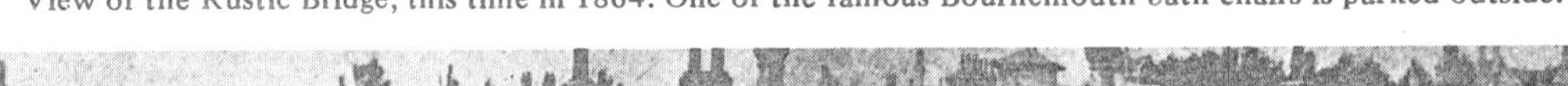
View of the Rustic Bridge, this time in 1864. One of the famous Bournemouth bath chairs is parked outside.

Gervis place and St. Peter's Church in 1874. Number 1 Westover Villas is on the corner, the present site of Austin Reed.

This is the foot of Boscombe hill as it appeared in 1862. The site of Boscombe Gardens is on the right and the Linden Hall Hydro on the left. Linden Hall Hydro was originally 'Linden Lea', a ten-roomed house which was erected in the late 1880's.

Holdenhurst Village in 1900. This picturesque little village still retains its charm. The Parish Church has changed little and the cottages can still be identified.

Throop in 1900. Near to Holdenhurst, on the outskirts of Bournemouth, Throop has not changed a great deal, although the cottage has gone.

Boscombe Spa in 1876. The little thatched shack enclosed a mineral spring, which was known as the 'Spa'. The aerated water from here was popular on Bournemouth tables during the 1870's. The large building on the horizon is the Boscombe Spa Hotel built in 1874, which is now part of the Chine Hotel.

SOFTLAW'S

LANSDOWNE HOTEL,

BOURNEMOUTH,

For FAMILIES and GENTLEMEN.

In the Immediate Vicinity of the PINE WOODS and EAST CLIFF.

The Private Suites of Apartments are Replete with every Comfort.

FIRST-CLASS CUISINE, EN PENSION.

SOUPS SENT OUT.

C. T. SOFTLAW, Proprietor.

People

Mr. Joseph Cutler photographed with his friend Mr. George Fox, Bournemouth's first postmaster. Cutler was one of Bournemouth's well known entrepreneurs of the second half of the 19th century. He had many business interests and was responsible for a number of property developments. He made and lost a lot of money; after one disastrous financial episode, he emigrated to Australia, where he remade his fortune.

Sir Merton Russell-Cotes, one of Bournemouth's most public-spirited citizens, photographed with his wife. He was proprietor of the Royal Bath Hotel and was also, by invitation, one-time mayor of Bournemouth. His home, East Cliff Hall, was given to the Borough for use as a museum and art gallery, and is today the Russell-Cotes Museum.

Mr. Robert Day, the Town's first photographer.

Joseph Cutler's portrait in tiles, which he had placed on one of his developments known as Joseph's Terrace, 216-236 Old Christchurch Road, which he built in about 1880.

Fashionable residencies of Bournemouth during the latter part of the 19th century and the early part of the 20th century employed large numbers of domestic staff. The "Upstairs, Downstairs" facets of life at the time are seen on these two pages. On the left, the maids and the gardener of the Reverend Cole of Westbourne and above, the Lady of the House, dressed in the elegant fashion of the turn of the century. The Cole household were ardently interested in photography and many of the photographs in this book are the result of their enthusiasm. Thus, due to the activities of these early amateur photographers, we have a valuable and interesting record of all aspects of life in Bournemouth at the turn of the century, including the servants shown here, who were rarely photographed.

The blacksmith and farrier, Henry Dyer, with his family, photographed at Wyndham Road, Springbourne, in 1898.

Left: A family group photograph, taken in 1912.

Children and parrot. An Edwardian childhood.

Children with a pull-chair.

The divers and crew of the dredger which was responsible for clearing the drain outlets in Bournemouth in 1927. In the divers suit is Mick Newman, who retired at the ripe old age of 82!

Members of the family of the Reverend Cole, photographed at the turn of the century, by another member of the family, with a portable glass plate camera.

Mr. (later Sir) Dan Godfrey, conductor of the Municipal Orchestra.

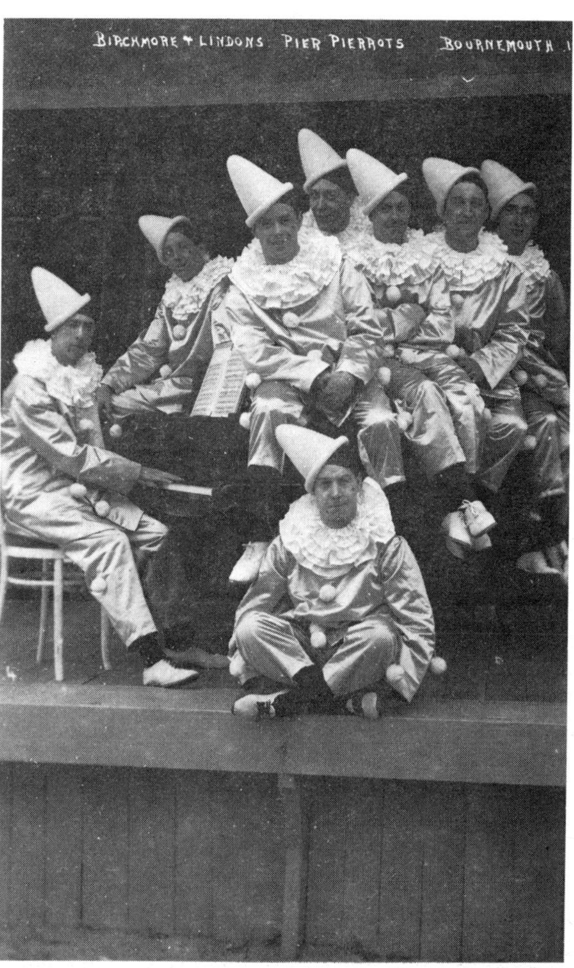

Birchmore and Linden's Pier Pierrots in 1915. They were a popular attraction at Bournemouth Pier until about 1920.

Dan Godfrey conducting his "band" at the Winter Gardens in 1903.

Members of the Reverend Cole's family at Westbourne in the 1890's. The summer dress and hats of the party make a charming picture; note the camera on the lap of the young lady in front.

The Reverend Cole of Westbourne in the 1890's. Return from tropical climates is indicated by his head-gear.

An Edwardian family group of the well-known Bournemouth family the Exton's, whose members achieved success in many spheres. On the right is Mr. Leo Exton of Westover Ice Rink and garages. They were connected for many years with the Linden Hall Hydro.

Top: A member of the Cole family, dressed for a wedding in the 1890's.

Right: A Victorian *'Carte de Visite'.* "Grandpa aged 89".

Left: A young Victorian girl on one of the many farms on the outskirts of Bournemouth.

The Vicar of Holy Trinity Church in Old Christchurch Road, the Reverend A. S. V. Blunt, M. A.

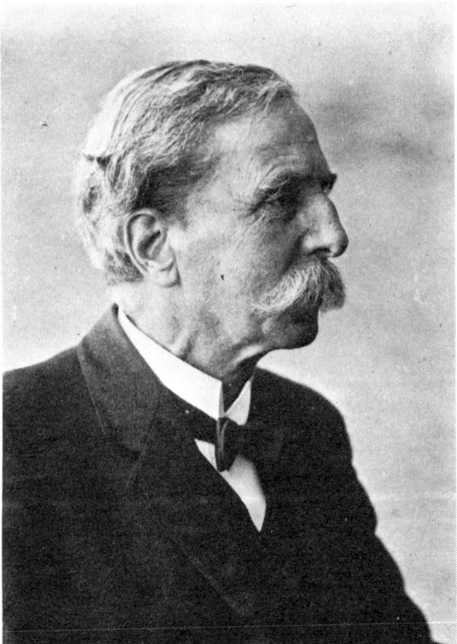

Robert Day's son, who continued his business until the 1920's.

"Chang" the Chinese giant who in his time was one of the town's most colourful and well-known personalities. His real name was Chang Woo Gow. He retired to Bournemouth with suspected tuberculosis in 1890 aged 49. He bought a spacious house "Moyuen" in Southcote Road where he lived with his Australian-born wife and their two teenage sons, who were both of normal height, unlike their father who was 8 feet tall and weighed 26 stone. The Victorian fascination for people with strange customs and the mystery of the Orient knew no bounds. Chang appeared all over Europe and in exhibitions in London. The sudden death of his wife was followed by his own, of a broken heart, on 5th November 1893. A vast concourse of residents attended his funeral at the Central Cemetry, Wimborne Road. His coffin measured 8'4" x 2'6".

Above: The Tuckton Football Club in 1907 with the founder, Count Vladimir Tchertkoff (arrowed). In front on the right is Vladimir Tchertkoff (junior). Tchertkoff was literary executor of Tolstoy.

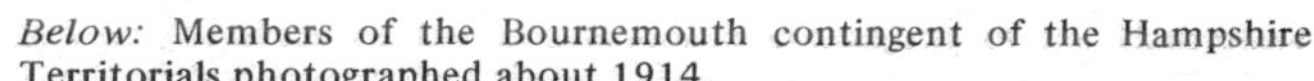

Left: A rifleman of the local 19th Hants Rifle Volunteer Corps in 1860.

Below: Members of the Bournemouth contingent of the Hampshire Territorials photographed about 1914.

This young subaltern escorts his mother and sister around the local camp in 1900.

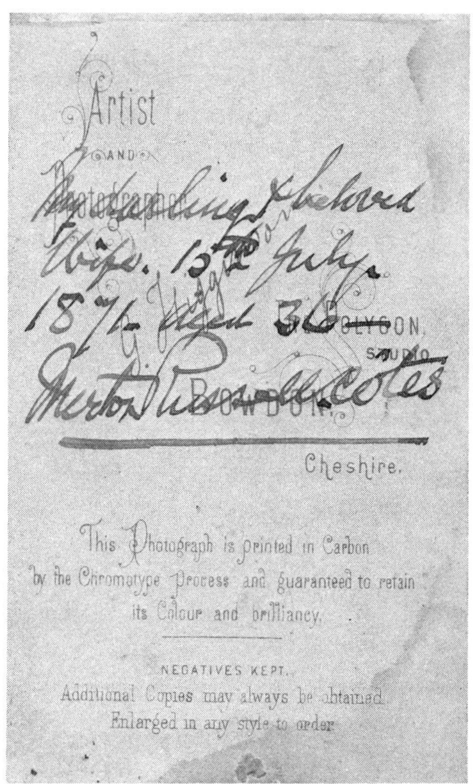

Russell-Cotes Museum photographed when it was East Cliff Hall, the home of Sir Merton Russell-Cotes.

Recreation

Bournemouth Pier Approach c. 1890 with a large crowd watching a Punch and Judy show - a very popular entertainment at that time, in the foreground. By a strange coincidence, the photograph on the right (taken some years later) was not only taken from the same spot, but also at the same time of day. Notice the clock.

"Everything is lovely, wish you were here". Bournemouth about 1912.

Looking east towards Bournemouth Pier Approach. This photograph, taken about 1912, shows the original Bournemouth Baths which at that time were called Sydenham's Baths and Reading Rooms.

Listening to the band under the awning gantry. Bournemouth 1898.

Promenading on the pier in 1899.

The Beach Minstrels, one of the many beach entertainments, popular around the turn of the century. The beach photographer's stand and camera can be clearly seen, as can the ice cream kiosk.

Two photographs of roller skating on Bournemouth Pier. The pier had a special deck built for the purpose, which was opened in 1898 by the Lord Mayor of London, Geoffrey Truscott. Similar facilities were also made available at Boscombe Pier, and several hours were reserved for skating on Tuesday and Friday afternoons. Roller skating became a national craze.

Young Neville Pike, aged about 3 when this photograph was taken in 1920, riding one of the ponies which were hired out by Mr. McGill. The ponies, 10 in number, were hitched to a rail running down the slipway to the sands on the east side of the pier.

Below: The beach banana- seller.

Above right: The fruit and lemonade kiosk on the east side of the slipway of Bournemouth Pier, taken about 1914. These kiosks, owned by the Bournemouth Corporation, were put up for tender each year. Pictured are Mr. Harold (Jack) Pike and his wife Annie, who leased the kiosk from before the first war until the early 1930's. His father, Charles Pike, built a large part of the Lansdowne Park Estate.

Right: The lemonade kiosk in 1929.

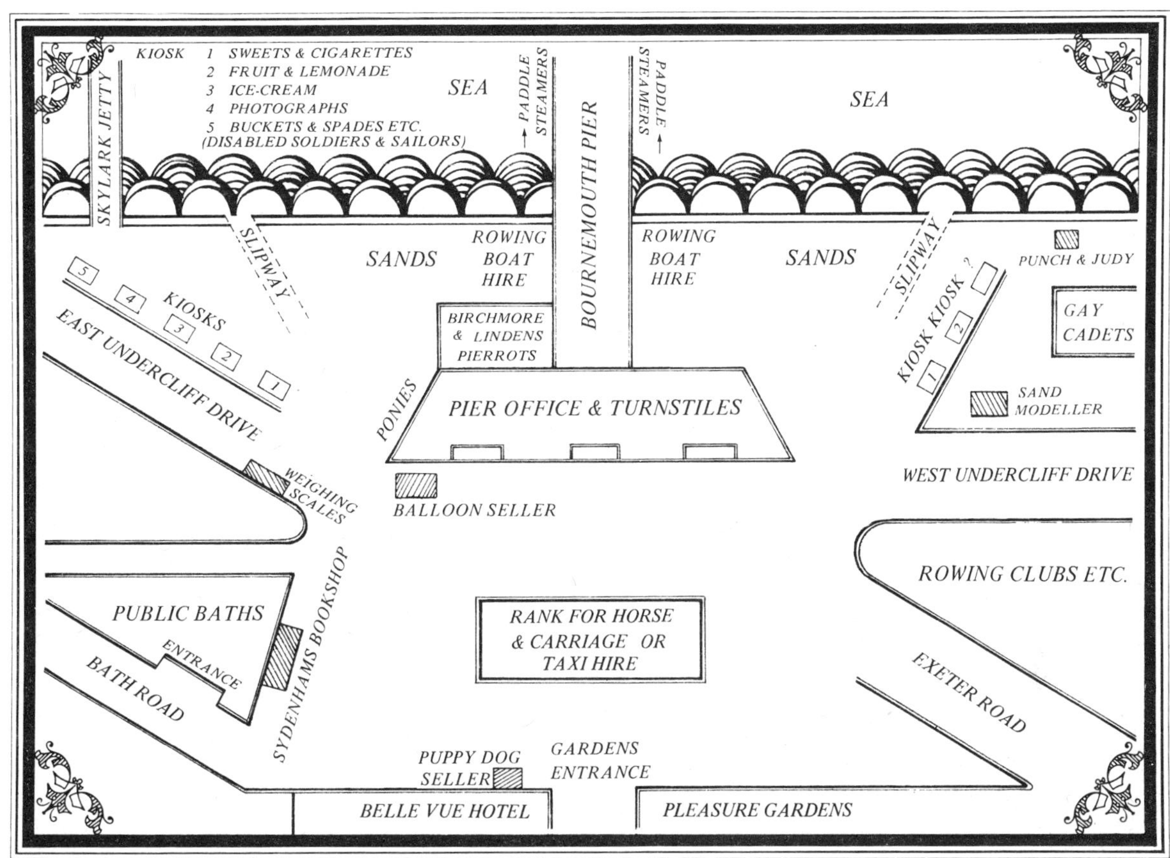

Some of the kiosks on the east slipway near the pier.

The scene on the beach from the East Cliff during the Regatta of 1890.

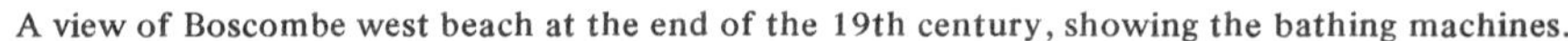

A view of Boscombe west beach at the end of the 19th century, showing the bathing machines.

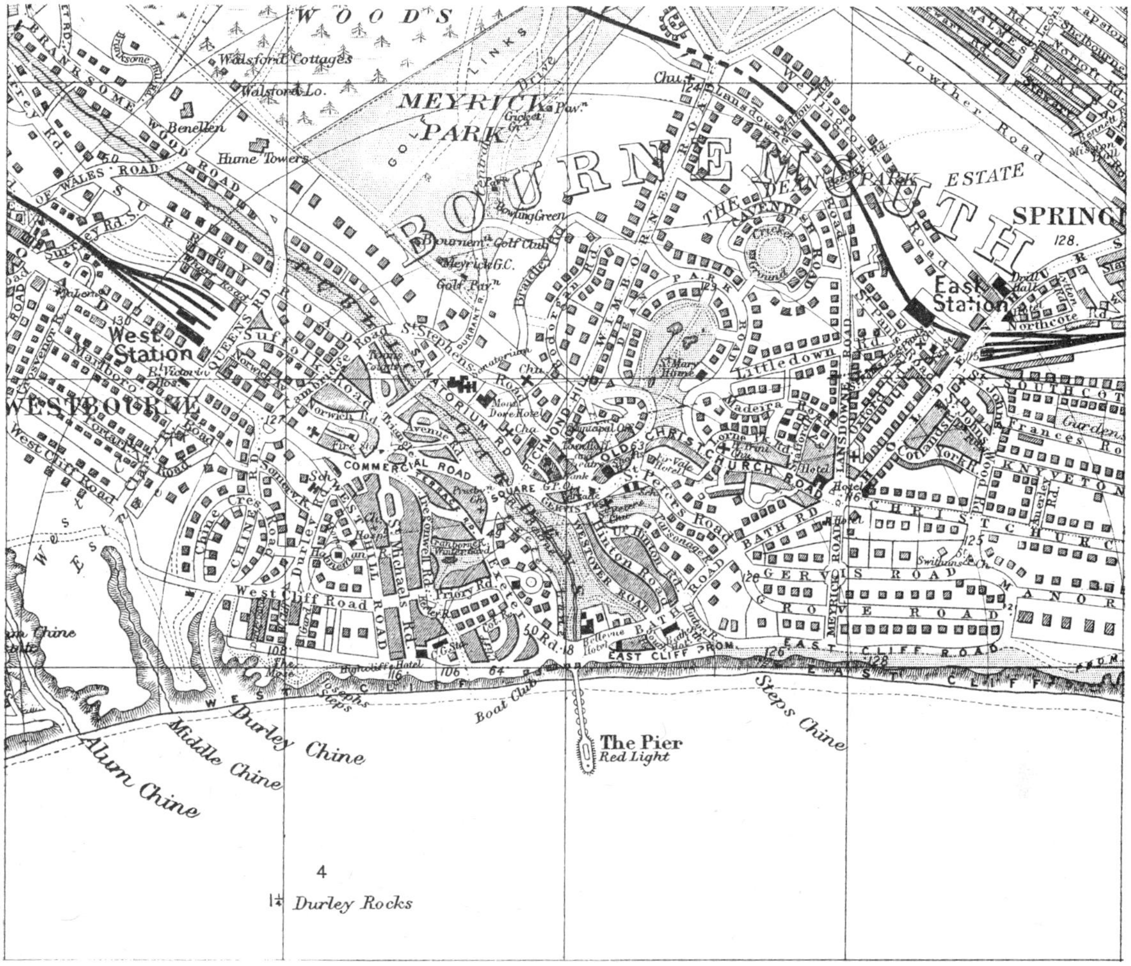

An early map of Bournemouth dated 1901.

The cliffs and esplanade were always in danger of collapsing. This photograph of Southbourne beach, taken about 1900, shows the houses, built in 1888, which were abandoned due to the ever-encroaching sea, which had already destroyed parts of the promenade and sea wall.

On the beach in Edwardian Bournemouth.

Tea on the beach on Regatta Day 1908.

The beach Punch and Judy show appearing at the Childrens Fete in Meyrick Park.

Bournemouth was a very popular resort in Victorian and Edwardian times as this early photograph testifies.

The Pierrots, performing on the beach before an appreciative audience in 1900.

On a day-trip to Bournemouth in the late 1920's.

The east beach in 1932, with the Punch and Judy show, a delight for children of many ages.

Shrimping !

A crowded beach in front of Sydenham's Baths and Reading Rooms, which stood on the site of the present Pier Approach Baths. The photograph was probably taken about 1890.

Enjoying the sands at the entrance to Branksome Chine in 1912.

"Anyone for the Skylark?" - a 1925 version.

Y.M.C.A. BOATHOUSE
VICTORIA

A magnificent group photograph of supporters at the Y.M.C.A. Boathouse on the west beach in 1895.

Redhill Tea Gardens in 1900. With the straightening of the river, this part is now a flat waste ground, and a caravan park. The Tea Garden was on the Bournemouth side of the Redhill Ferry to West Parley and operated until the late 1930's.

An afternoon stroll through the lower gardens in 1910. The roof of the Mont Dore Hotel (now the Town Hall) can be seen above the trees on the left, and the spire of St. Peter's Church on the right.

A fashionable garden party in a local vicarage in the summer of 1898.

"The Mirror Kid". The second-prize winner in the fancy dress competition of the Children's Festival in June 1909.

The Redhill Tea Gardens in 1913.

A barrel of Edwardian fun.

A picnic in a local hay field about 1900.

Over the stile with Grandma!

H.R.H. Prince Henry of Battenberg, photographed in 1894 on the first tee at Meyrick Park Golf Links with the Mayor, Merton Russell-Cotes.

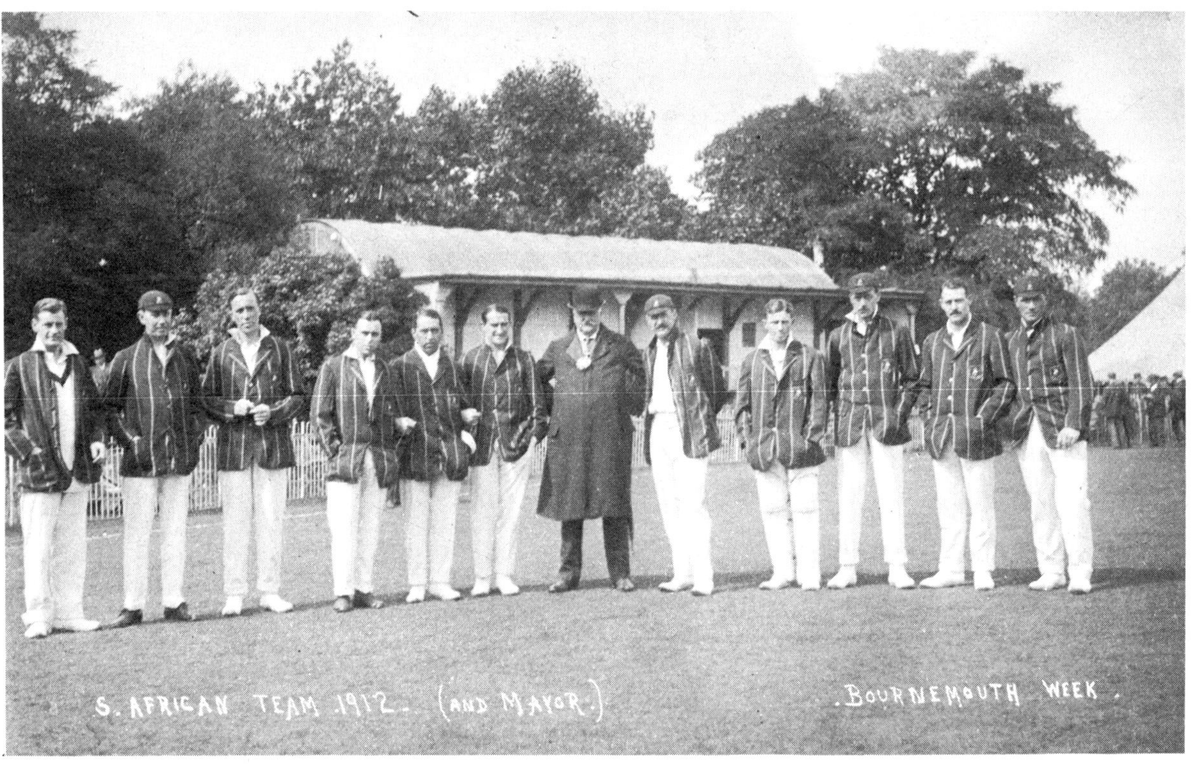

The South African cricket team with the Mayor of Bournemouth during Cricket Week at Dean Park Ground in 1912.

Anyone for tennis?

Horseshoe Common at the turn of the century.

Rowing in the Bay.

Sailing on the Bourne.

The Tea Rooms at Wick Ferry looking to Southbourne Bank. They were constructed on the hull of a paddle steamer.

Entertainment

The Winter Gardens, c. 1900.

The young Mr. Dan Godfrey with the Royal Italian Band in 1893 at the Winter Gardens. Sinc

cians were all former members of the Italian army, they were entitled to wear military uniforms.

The exterior of the old Winter Gardens photographed about 1900.

Known to some as the "hot house", the interior of the old Winter Gardens photographed in 1900.

A corner of the Grand Hall of the Theatre Royal in 1900, a most popular place for afternoon tea. Built on the site of Albert House, it was for a time the home of ex-Queen-Marie-Amelia (1782-1866), widow of Louis Philippe of France. Opened in 1882, it was used from 1887-1892 as Bournemouth's second Town Hall. It again continued as a theatre until after World War II. Oscar Wilde lectured here.

Theatre Royal,

Proprietors—
Mr. H. H. MORELL, Mr. Fredk. MOUILLOT, and Messrs. DAVID ALLEN & SONS.

Manager—Mr. CLYDE MEYNELL.
Acting Manager—Mr. GEO. CLARKSON.

THE PRETTIEST AND . .
MOST COMFORTABLE THEATRE
IN THE SOUTH OF ENGLAND.
* * *

Bournemouth.

Open Every Evening, AT POPULAR PRICES with . . FIRST-CLASS COMPANIES ONLY.

Telegrams:—"THEATRE, BOURNEMOUTH."
Telephone No. 7, BOURNEMOUTH.

For particulars of Current Performances see Newspaper Advertisements and Theatre Day Bills.

Frequent Matinees. Frequent Matinees. Frequent Matinees.

Theatre Royal, Dublin.
Mr. H. H. Morell and Mr. Fredk. Mouillot, Managing Directors
Theatre Royal, Belfast.
Grand Opera House, Belfast.
Mr. H. H. Morell and Mr. F. Mouillot, Directors
Opera House, Cork.
Mr. H. H. Morell & Mr. Fredk. Mouillot, Directors.

Grand Theatre, Southampton.

Grand Theatre, Swansea.
Grand Theatre, Margate.
Queen's Theatre, Leeds.
Mr. H. H. Morell and Mr. Fredk. Mouillot, Proprietors.
Queen's Theatre, London, N.
Metropole Theatre, Glasgow.

Mr. MORELL, Mr. MOUILLOT and DAVID ALLEN & SONS, Proprietors. Mr. CLYDE MEYNELL, Manager.

Mr. H. H. MORELL and Mr. Fredk. MOUILLOT, Proprietors.

The Theatre Royal as it is today.

HIPPODROME

BOSCOMBE.

6.10 Twice Nightly. **8.15**

Varieties. **Revues.**

CHANGE OF PROGRAMME EVERY WEEK.

Prices of Admission—Boxes, 15/- and 10/6 ; Orchestral Stalls, 2/- ; Stalls, 1/6.
(Booked in advance without extra charge)
Balcony, 9d. ; Gallery, 6d. (Tax extra).

BOOKING OFFICE OPEN FROM 11 A.M. TO 9 P.M. **TELEPHONE 706.**

The Grand Theatre, Boscombe, first opened in 1905 as the Boscombe Hippodrome. Among the artists that appeared here were Buffalo Bill and Henry Irving.

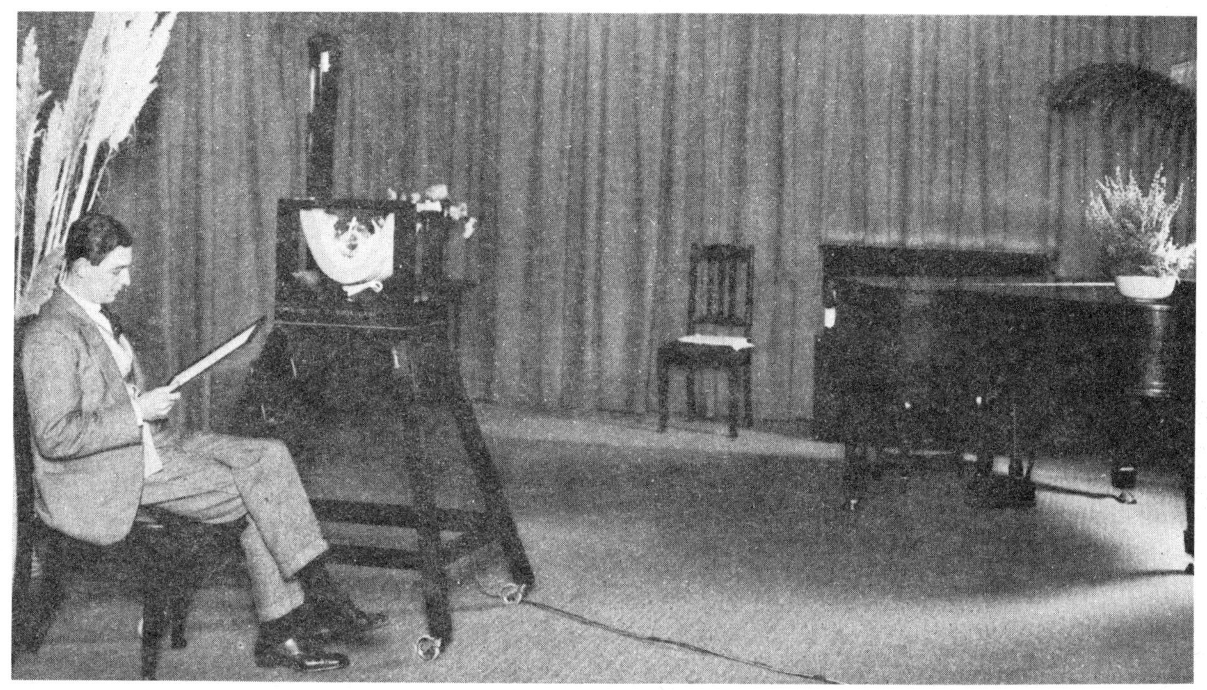

Bertram Fryer at the microphone in the BBC Radio Studio in Holdenhurst Road.

72/73 Holdenhurst Road. The local broadcasting station was established on the first floor.

Events

The salute to Queen Victoria on her Golden Jubilee.

H.R.H. Prince Henry of Battenberg arriving at the Royal Bath Hotel photographed during his visit to Bournemouth in 1894. He died two years later during the Zulu war as a serving officer.

The Lord Mayor of London opening the new pedestrian and roller skating deck of the pier on the 5th June 1909. He is pictured here on the SS Majestic tied up alongside.

An enthusiastic crowd follows General Booth, founder of the Salvation Army, as his motorcade drives through The Square on the 26th August, 1906.

The huge crowd in The Square gather for the Proclamation of the Accession of King Edward VII on the 2nd January 1901.

The Centenary Fetes of 1910 to celebrate the founding of Bournemouth, lasted for over five days. One of the events was a competition for the best carnival float, some of which were brought from Italy. This one was entitled "Cock of the Day".

Bournemouth Centenary Fetes.
The Arcade. No. 6.

OLD CHRISTCHURCH ROAD
BOURNEMOUTH CENTENARY FETES JULY 1910 8

Bournemouth Centenary Fetes.
The Battle of Flowers. No. 38.

Colonel Cody, one of the aviators at the International Aviation Meeting at Bournemouth in July 1910. Colonel Samuel Franklin Cody (1861-1913), a British aviator, was born in U.S.A. but became a naturalised British subject. He was the first man to fly in Great Britain making a flight of 27 minutes in October 1908 in the first practical British flying machine of his own make. He was killed whilst flying in 1913.

Although this photograph is labelled "The first airship over Bou
in fact flown by William E. McArdle, almost two months earlier

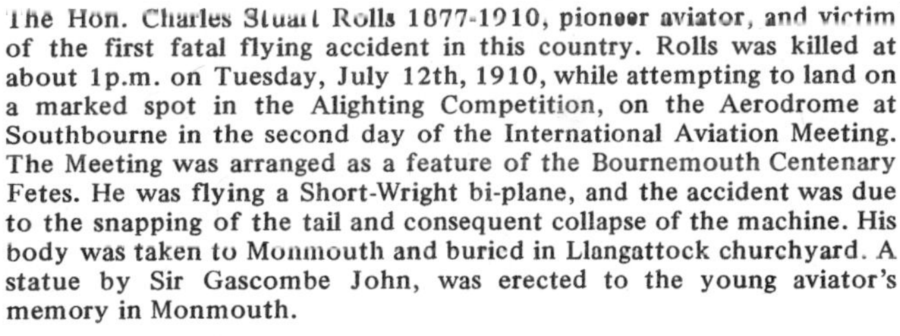

The Hon. Charles Stuart Rolls 1877-1910, pioneer aviator, and victim of the first fatal flying accident in this country. Rolls was killed at about 1p.m. on Tuesday, July 12th, 1910, while attempting to land on a marked spot in the Alighting Competition, on the Aerodrome at Southbourne in the second day of the International Aviation Meeting. The Meeting was arranged as a feature of the Bournemouth Centenary Fetes. He was flying a Short-Wright bi-plane, and the accident was due to the snapping of the tail and consequent collapse of the machine. His body was taken to Monmouth and buried in Llangattock churchyard. A statue by Sir Gascombe John, was erected to the young aviator's memory in Monmouth.

l dated July 11th, 1910, the first aircraft over Bournemouth was y.

One of the competitors at the Bournemouth International Aviation Meeting of 1910.

Bournemouth Aviation Meeting.
Col. Cody. Erecting his Machine.
No. 66.

Bournemouth Aviation Meeting.
Barnes. Preparing for a Flight.
No. 73.

Bournemouth Aviation Meeting,
The Hon. C.S. Rolls in the air.
No. 62

"DAILY MAIL" WATERPLANE CIRCUIT, 1912.
70 H.P. HENRY FARMAN WATERPLANE.

"DAILY MAIL" WATERPLANE CIRCUIT, 1912.
70 H.P. HENRY FARMAN WATERPLANE.

HMS Dreadnought the flag ship of the Home Fleet in Bournemouth Bay, July 1907.

The Home Fleet in Bournemouth Bay, July 1907.

Civic luncheon given by the Mayor and Town Council of Bournemouth to the Officers, Captains and Commanders of the Home Fleet in the Winter Gardens on Saturday, 27th July, 1907.

Crowds on the pier watching the arrival of the ships of the Home Fleet in Bournemouth Bay, on July 26th, 1907.

Trade

Notwithstanding Bournemouth is still in its infancy, it is well supplied with provisions and necessaries of all kinds, several shops having been already opened; and the place within an easy reach of the plentifully supplied and cheap market of Poole, with which there are facilities for communications at all hours of the day, nö difficulty whatever is experienced.

First Bournemouth Guide, 1840.

A view of Old Christchurch Road, in 1921, Bournemouth's principal trading area.

Herbert Rigler's, Corn Merchant's shop on the corner of Lesley and Wimborne Roads, photographed about 1914. The site is now occupied by Sainsbury's supermarket.

A baker's boy in the early part of the century, delivering supplies to a grocery and provisions store in Pokesdown.

M. H. COX,

Family Grocer, Tea Dealer and Wine Merchant,

BOURNEMOUTH.

PICKLES, FISH SAUCES, FOREIGN FRUITS AND SPICES.

BRITISH WINES.

FINE FOREIGN CIGARS, FANCY SNUFFS.

WAX, SPERM, MARGARINE, AND COMPOSITE CANDLES.

DRIED PICKLED TONGUES AND HOME-CURED HAMS.

Agent to the European and Colonial Wine Company, Pall Mall, London.

LUNCHEON AND REFRESHMENT ROOMS.

J. MILES,

BREAD AND BISCUIT BAKER,

Pastry Cook and Confectioner,

SOUTH BOURNE TERRACE, BOURNEMOUTH.

Jellies, Blanc Manges, and Choice Confectionery.

Wedding Cakes on the shortest notice.

FANCY BREAD, BISCUITS, &c., OF EVERY DESCRIPTION.

Genuine Home-made and Digestive Bread.

BRITISH WINES.

The premises of L. F. King, Bournemouth's principal baker, at 214 Holdenhurst Road. This photograph which dates to the early years of this century, shows both the horse-drawn and hand delivery carts.

1900 advertisement for Isaac & Co. Ltd., the forerunner of the renowned Malmesbury and Parsons Dairies, now Unigate.

The interior of King's bakery in Holdenhurst Road.

The Royal Arcade, Boscombe, in the early 1900's.

Holdenhurst Road in 1905. The entrance to the original fire station can be seen on the right, behind the tree.

DORSET PLACE,
BOURNEMOUTH.

MRS. GAVIN'S
FINE ARTS REPOSITORY,

DEPOT FOR LIBRARY COMPANY,
(LIMITED)

(Subscribers to this Library can be Transferred to any Depot of the Library Company.)

ON SALE.

THEOLOGICAL AND OTHER BOOKS

PUBLISHED BY
MESSRS. MASTERS, PARKER, RIVINGTON, AND THE S.P.C.K.

DE LA RUE'S STATIONERY.

Agent for Winsor and Newton's Drawing and Illuminating Materials.

Repository for the Sale of Works for Charitable Purposes.

Bibles, Prayer Books, &c.

Guide Books, Maps, and Views of Bournemouth and the neighbourhood.

THE "TIMES" LENT OUT TO READ.

PUBLICATIONS SUPPLIED.

LEVERETT and FRYE,
THE SQUARE,
BOURNEMOUTH,
SUPPLY

Groceries and Provisions

OF THE FINEST QUALITY, FROM ANY
CO-OPERATIVE STORE LIST.

PATENT MEDICINES, PERFUMERY, &c., &c.

AGENTS FOR

W. & A. GILBEY'S
WINES and SPIRITS.

MOET'S, CLIQUET'S, ROEDERER'S
AND ALL OTHER BEST BRAND CHAMPAGNES AT STORE PRICES.

Orders Collected and Goods Delivered FREE.
Westbourne and Parkstone Wednesdays and Saturdays.

Not all trading was done in shops. Here a travelling pet shop is parked in Bournemouth Square in about 1905. On the side of the cart is the sign *"Dealer in Caged Birds, Fancy and Toy Dogs"*.

CHARLES FOX,

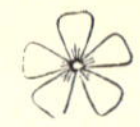

TELEGRAPHIC ADDRESS—
"FOX, JEWELLER, BOURNEMOUTH."
TELEPHONE 72X.

20, Old Christchurch Rd.,
Bournemouth (Near Arcade).

Diamond Merchant, Jeweller & Silversmith.

Watches, Clocks and Jewellery Repaired on the Premises by Experienced Workmen at moderate Charges. All Work Guaranteed

The Best Assortment in Bournemouth of Engagement, Wedding and Birthday Gifts.

Visitors will find a Large and Varied Assortment in all kinds of Jewellery and Silver Goods.

Specialities:
Bournemouth Hot Water Jugs, from 11/6. Souvenir Spoons, Solid Silver, 5/6.
Diamonds and Gems Re-mounted in up-to-date Styles. Designs and Estimates FREE.
Old Gold, Silver and Gems Bought for Cash, Highest prices given.

TRY FOX'S "EUREKA" PLATE POLISH IN SCREW STOPPER BOTTLES, 1/- & 1/6.

Bournemouth Arcade in 1908. A major shopping precinct of Edwardian times.

Bright's Stores, 1900.

DEVONSHIRE CREAM, JUNKETS, &c.

ISAAC & CO., Est. 1876.

Malmesbury Dairies,

BOURNEMOUTH, BOSCOMBE, & WESTBOURNE.

Central Office:
23, **OLD CHRISTCHURCH ROAD** (First Door East of Arcade).

Head Office: 27, ASHLEY ROAD, BOSCOMBE.
Telephone No. 733.

Westbourne and Branksome Park Branch:
3, PARK TERRACE, WESTBOURNE.
Telephone No. 248.

Milk, Cream, Butter, and Eggs delivered to every part of the Borough twice daily.

Obtained from Farms on Lord Malmesbury's Estate.
FREQUENTLY INSPECTED BY LOCAL MEDICAL MEN.

Dash,

Practical Hatter,

51, Old Christchurch Road,

BOURNEMOUTH.

DASH, for Hat Making, or Blocking, or Lining.

DASH, for Servants' Livery Hats.

DASH, for Umbrellas and Hosiery.

DASH, for Umbrella Recovering or Repairing.

DASH, for Lightest Hats in the World.

THE NORTH FRONT OF THE ARCADE.

BRIGHT  & SON,

The Arcade, Bournemouth.

By Special Appointment.

Booksellers and Stationers,

Dealers in Fancy Goods, China and Glass, and Oriental Bric-a-Brac,

IMPORTERS OF BERLIN WOOLS AND ART NEEDLEWORK,

DEALERS IN FOREIGN STAMPS.

THE LARGEST, BEST, & MOST CENTRAL CIRCULATING LIBRARY
TWO SETS FOR 21s. A YEAR.

THE BEST GUIDE TO BOURNEMOUTH,
With Map and Photo Illustrations, price 1s.

The New Index of Bournemouth,
Price 1s.

The Best View Book of Bournemouth,
Just Published, price 1s.

ARTISTS' OIL AND WATER COLOURS.
Threepence in the Shilling Discount for Cash.

Telegraphic Address: BRIGHT, ARCADE, BOURNEMOUTH.

The Criterion Arcade (then Town Hall Avenue) decorated for the 1910 Centenary celebrations.

An early photograph of Offers, the tobacconist's shop in Bournemouth Arcade.

VISITORS TO BOURNEMOUTH

SHOULD VISIT THIS ESTABLISHMENT.

NEARLY

FOUR ACRES

OF

MAGNIFICENT SHOWROOMS

BRIM FULL OF

UP-TO-DATE GOODS

suitably arranged for the comfort and convenience of customers, and form a

GRAND ARCADE

FROM THE

QUADRANT HOUSE

(ENTRANCE THROUGH THE VARIOUS ROOMS) TO THE

OLD POST OFFICE BUILDINGS.

ENTRANCE — **Quadrant House,** OLD CHRISTCHURCH ROAD.

EXIT — **The Quadrant,** OR VICE VERSA.

HAVE YOU VISITED

TAYLOR'S

China Rooms. ::

OPENING OF :: ::

New SHOW ROOM

Special Display of LATEST NOVELTIES in ::

China and Glass.

INSPECTION INVITED.

TAYLOR'S CHINA ROOMS,
66, OLD CHRISTCHURCH ROAD, BOURNEMOUTH.

Top: Beales Fancy Fair and Oriental House on the corner of Old Christchurch Road and Hinton Road in 1900. The store was founded by J. E. Beale in 1886.

Left: A view of the Toy Department at Beales in 1900, a virtual treasure-house of juvenalia.

Right: Another view of the Toy Department at Beales in 1900.

Left: Beales Fancy Fair and Oriental House, 1900.

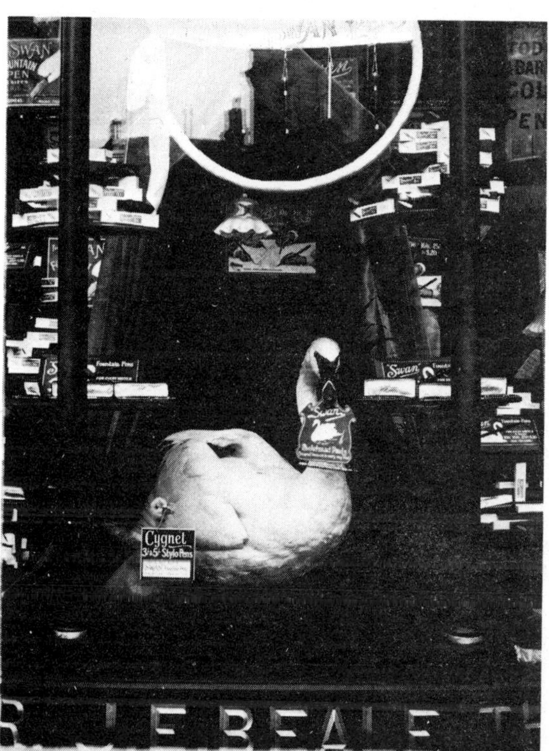

The Swan advertisement show window at Beales.

The interior of the Oriental department at Beales.

Right: Another of the fabulous window displays at Beales Fancy Fair in 1900.

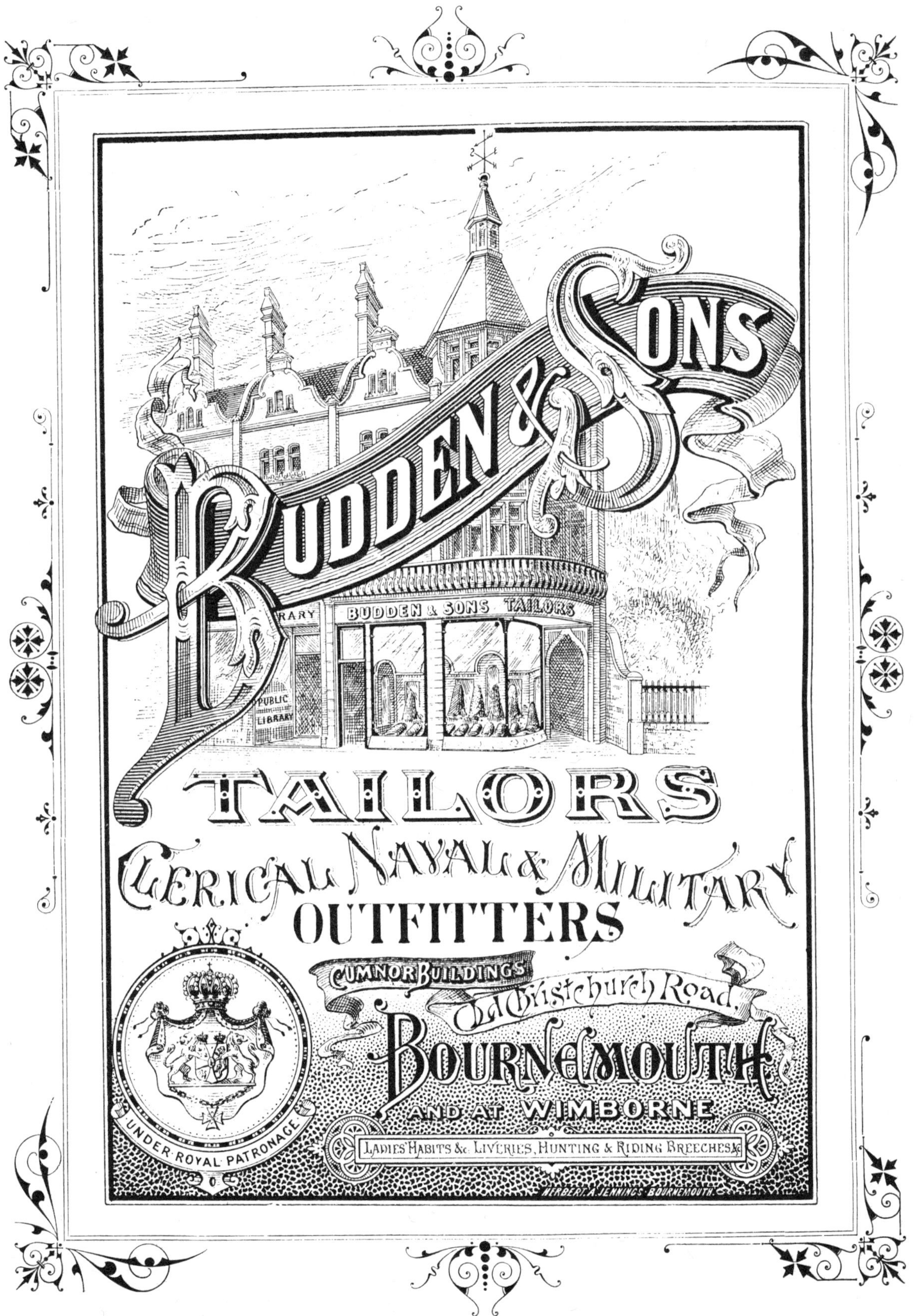
BUDDEN & SONS
BUDDEN & SONS TAILORS
PUBLIC LIBRARY
TAILORS
CLERICAL NAVAL & MILITARY
OUTFITTERS
UNDER ROYAL PATRONAGE
CUMNOR BUILDINGS
Old Christchurch Road,
BOURNEMOUTH
AND AT WIMBORNE
LADIES' HABITS &c. LIVERIES, HUNTING & RIDING BREECHES &c.
HERBERT A. JENNINGS BOURNEMOUTH

BIRMINGHAM HOUSE,

ALUMHURST ROAD,

WESTBOURNE, BOURNEMOUTH.

ELECTRIC BELLS SUPPLIED & FITTED BY EXPERIENCED WORKMEN.

ESTIMATES FOR ALL KINDS OF GREENHOUSES AND ALTERATIONS FOR SAME ON THE MOST MODERN APPROVED PRINCIPLE.

C. WILLS & SONS,

General and Furnishing Ironmongers,

Shoeing & Jobbing Smiths,

GAS, HOT AND COLD WATER, AND RANGE FITTERS,

Locksmiths & Bell Hangers, Oil Merchants, &c.

All kinds of Repairs done on the Premises.

C. W. has 30 Years' Practical Experience in the above Branches.

Range, Grate, and Chimney-Piece Department.

C. WILLS & SONS have an extensive stock on view in their

SEAMOOR SHOW ROOMS,

And invite the inspection of Architects, Builders, and others, who desire to make a selection.

NORMANHURST, BOURNEMOUTH WEST.

SCHOOL FOR GIRLS. Principal: MISS EVERARD.

SEE ADVERTISEMENT IN "BOURNEMOUTH VISITORS' DIRECTORY."

GO TO

NORMAN'S

FOR

BICYCLES.
TRICYCLES.
SEWING MACHINES.
KNITTING MACHINES.
PERAMBULATORS.
BASSINETTES.
INVALID WICKER AND BATH CHAIRS.
SPINAL CARRIAGES.
INVALID SELF-PROPELLING CHAIRS.
CARRYING CHAIRS, &c.
KNIFE CLEANERS.
WASHING MACHINES.
MANGLES.
WRINGERS.

ALL MACHINES MADE AND REPAIRED.

STOVING, ENAMELLING, NICKEL-PLATING.

ALL MACHINES LENT ON HIRE.

PLEASE SEND FOR LISTS.

---

500 IN STOCK.

CHEAPEST HOUSE IN THE TRADE.

J. S. NORMAN,

***Cycle Works,* 5, 6, & 7, The Quadrant, BOURNEMOUTH.**

(Close to St. Peter's Church and Post Office.)

Blacklock the chemist in the Square in about 1898. Founded in 1845, its patrons included Robert Louis Stevenson and Charles Darwin.

E. WORTH,

DISPENSING CHEMIST,

THE BOURNEMOUTH PHARMACY,

TOWN HALL, (Opposite the ARCADE,)

And at BOSCOMBE.

WORTH'S

BLACK CURRANT AND MARSHMALLOW

COUGH LOZENGES,

For Coughs, Colds, Hoarseness, Shortness of Breath, Irritation of the Throat, &c.

WORTH'S

PEPSINE DIGESTIVE CANDY.

(Registered.)

Digestive Candy has long been known as a valuable remedy for Indegestion, Flatulence, Acidity, &c. In this combination it is greatly improved by the addition of Pepsine, which is the active digestive principle of the gastric juice.

AGENT FOR

Schweppe's Mineral Waters.

Soda, Potash, and Seltzer Waters in Syphon Bottles.

Importer of Foreign Mineral Waters, Sponge, and Eau de Cologne.

"THE" CORN CURE.

SPEEDY AND EFFICACIOUS.

REMOVES CORNS AND WARTS WITHOUT PLASTER OR CUTTING.

Does not Relieve only, but REALLY CURES Hard or Soft Corns, Warts, Hardened Skin, &c.

PRICE 1/-; FREE BY POST, 1/1.

E. WORTH,

TELEPHONE NO. 10.
ESTABLISHED 1868.

PRESCRIPTIONS DISPENSED WITH SCRUPULOUS CARE.

: : Dispensing Chemist, : :

The Bournemouth Pharmacy,

OPPOSITE THE ARCADE.

THE BOURNEMOUTH PHARMACY. Mr. WORTH, Chemist.

Schweppe's Lithia, Potash and Soda Water, Lemonade, Malvern Seltzer.

Importer of Apenta, Hungadi, Carlsbad, Friedrichshall, Pullna, Seltzer, Vichy, and other Foreign Mineral Waters.

Soda, Potash and Seltzer Water supplied in Syphons.

ELASTIC BANDAGES, KNEE CAPS, STOCKINGS, &c.

HOT WATER BEDS,
PILLOWS, and CUSHIONS
LENT ON HIRE.

Patent Medicines and Proprietary Articles at Reduced Prices for Cash.

"THE" CORN CURE

Speedy and Efficacious.

REALLY CURES HARD OR SOFT CORNS, WARTS, HARDENED SKIN, etc.

PRICE 1/-. Free by Post.

Established 1865.

TO THE IMPERIAL FAMILY OF GERMANY
TO H.I.M. THE EMPRESS OF AUSTRIA
TO H.M. THE QUEEN OF SWEDEN

EST^D 1865

ARTHUR F. LAWRENCE,
(LATE DUNCAN,)
Dispensing & Family Chemist.
The Square, BOURNEMOUTH.

(Late Duncan,)

Telephone 91.
TELEGRAPHIC ADDRESS:
"Chemicus, Bournemouth."

DISPENSING CHYMIST,

THE SQUARE, BOURNEMOUTH.

A Full Stock of SPONGES, PERFUMERY, WASHING GLOVES and all TOILET ARTICLES.
INVALID REQUISITES of all kinds. Importer of all FOREIGN MINERAL WATERS.
Special Agent for "CAMWAL" TABLE WATERS.

Dispensing Department.

THIS Pharmacy has been re-built and additions made affording every facility for carrying on the important work of dispensing Physicians' Prescriptions. The Dispensing Department is underthe personal supervision of the Proprietor, and no efforts are spared in faithfully carrying out the Physicians' directions.

All prices charged are as low as possible, consistent with the quality and care given.
Medicines can be obtained at any hour, a Dispenser being in constant attendance.

SURGICAL APPLIANCES: Trusses, Belts, Elastic Stockings, Artificial Eyes, Limbs, &c.

N.B.—An Attendant to wait upon Ladies.

A funeral procession in Wimborne Road, Winton, in 1920.

C. DALES,

GREENWICH HOUSE,

WESTBOURNE.

Optician, Electrician,

Watch & Clock Maker,

Jeweller, and Photographer.

All kinds of Apparatus Repaired.

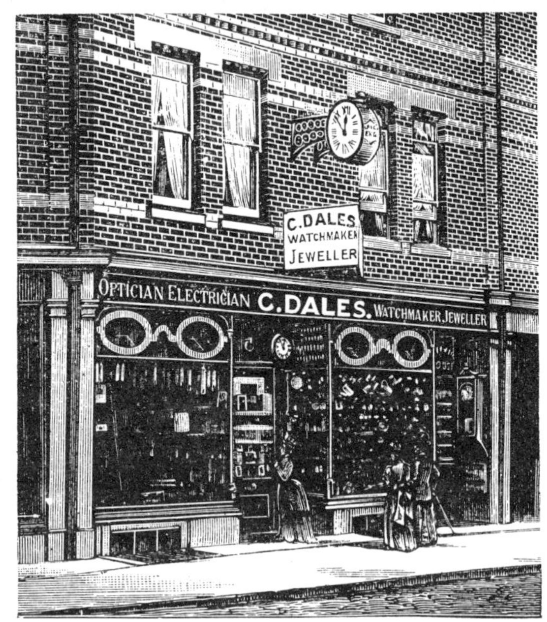

Speciality—any Oculist's Prescriptions accurately carried out.

C. DALES obtained a Diploma at the Spectacle Makers' Exhibition held in London.

The workshop of John Scott, undertaker, joiner and carpenter, at 121 Haviland Road. This photograph, taken in 1905, shows Ernest and John Scott standing on the left. The business later became Ernest John Scott Ltd., in 1936, and in 1940 changed its name to Derek S. Scott Ltd. Funerals were added as a sideline in 1937. Derek Scott Ltd. is now one of Bournemouth's foremost undertakers.

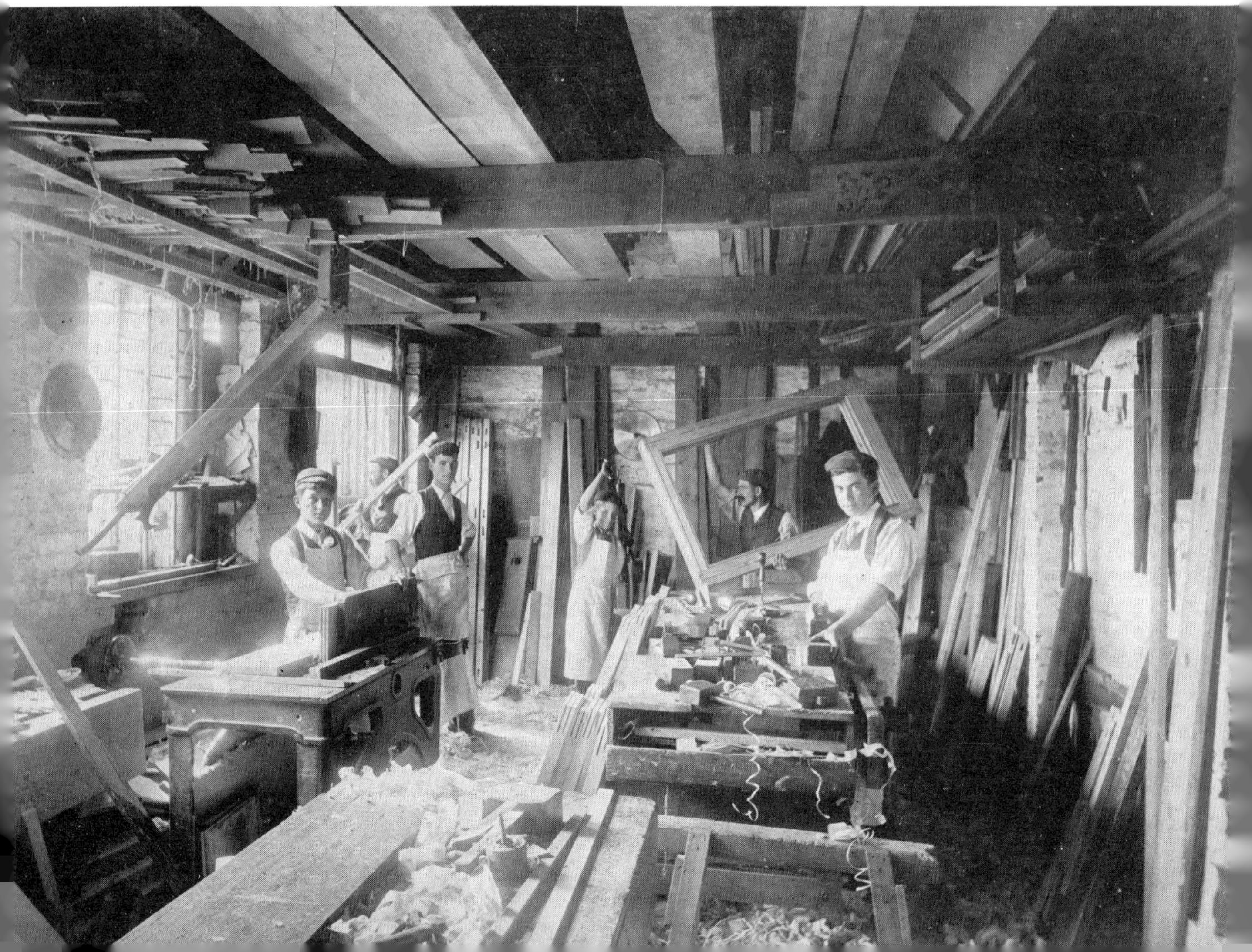

MUSSELWHITE & SIMPKINS,

Cabinet Makers and Upholsterers,

STEAM CABINET WORKS,
Avenue Lane, Bournemouth, W.

Bright's Stores, Ltd., Photo.

High Class Cabinet Work.

HARD WOOD JOINERY.

Shop Fittings. Air Tight Cases.

WOOD MANTEL PIECES.

BLINDS. CARPETS. LINOLEUMS.

ESTIMATES GIVEN.

The Bournemouth Brewery at 177 Holdenhurst Road, at the rear of the railway station, now Waverly House in 1905.

STURT, SONS, & TURNER,

House Furnishers, Auctioneers, House Agents, and Undertakers,

Dining,
Drawing,
Morning, and
Bedroom Suites,
Sideboards,
Dining Tables,
Dinner Wagons,
Overmantels,
Hall, and other
Furniture.

Chintzes,
Cretonnes,
Tapestries,
Serges,
Plushettes,
Carpets & Rugs,
Bedsteads,
and
Bedding.

These magnificent Showrooms are the largest in Bournemouth, covering an area of 35,000 square feet, and are replete with every Household Requisite.

Estimates given for Household Removals to all Parts.

Furniture stored in large Warehouses specially constructed for the purpose.

Intending Residents in Bournemouth are specially invited to communicate with S., S., & T., who will furnish them with a list of unoccupied Residences.

SHOW ROOMS, 29, Commercial Road, Bournemouth;

FACTORIES, AVENUE LANE, BOURNEMOUTH.

HOGG & SON,

11 & 13, *Commercial Road,*

Undertakers.

FUNERALS COMPLETELY FURNISHED
AT MOST MODERATE CHARGES.

Household Removals from all Parts.

ESTIMATES FREE OF CHARGE.

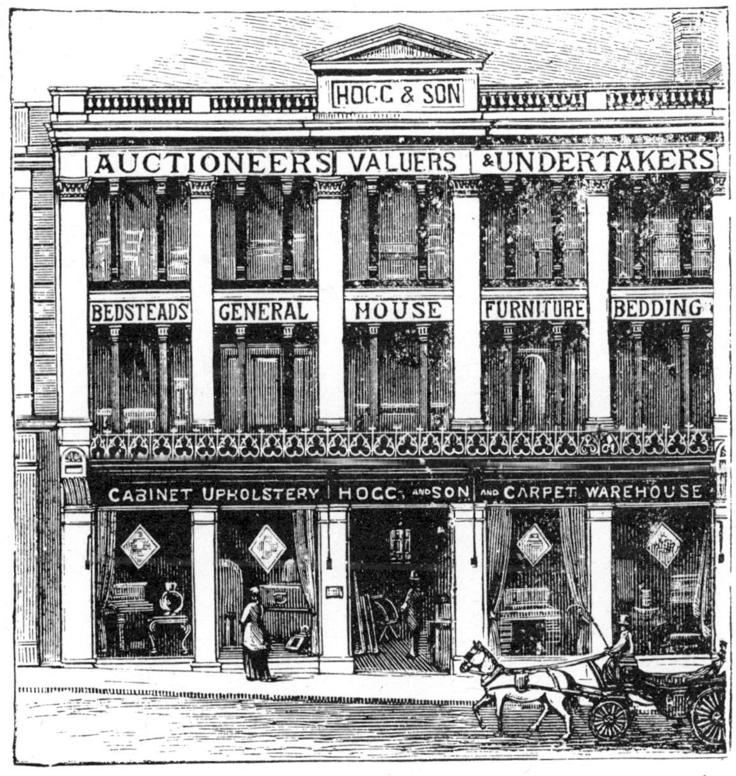

THE CHEAPEST AND BEST FURNISHING HOUSE.

IF YOU ARE PREPARED TO BUY FOR CASH,
Don't fail to make a call, as nothing short of Comparison can convince you that they can offer best value for Really Reliable Goods.

All kinds of Repairs, and all kinds of Bedding purified and re-made, on short notice, at the MOST MODERATE CHARGES, *by*

HOGG & SON, 11 & 13, Commercial Road, **BOURNEMOUTH.**

PERSONS DESIROUS OF INFORMATION RESPECTING

Furnished Houses or Lodgings

AT BOURNEMOUTH,

ARE RESPECTFULLY REQUESTED TO APPLY TO

W. E. REBBECK,

THE AUTHORIZED AGENT OF THE PRINCIPAL PROPRIETORS OF HOUSES AT THE ABOVE WATERING-PLACE.

Office of the Poole, Bournemouth, and South Coast
PRINTING TELEGRAPH COMPANY,
Open daily for the transmission of Messages.

ESTABLISHED 1865.

Messrs. HANKINSON & SON,

House and Estate Agents,

AUCTIONEERS AND SURVEYORS,

PUBLISH

Complete Monthly Property List,

And forward same free on application.

VALUATIONS FOR PROBATE, TRANSFER, & MORTGAGE.

LISTS OF APARTMENTS.

Agents for the Principal Insurance Offices.

Offices of the Branksome and Sandecotes Estates.

STOCK AND SHARE BROKERS.

Daily Official List and Leading Financial Papers Filed.

Address—

Richmond Chambers, Bournemouth.

Telegrams—"Richmond," Bournemouth. *Telephone No. 13.*

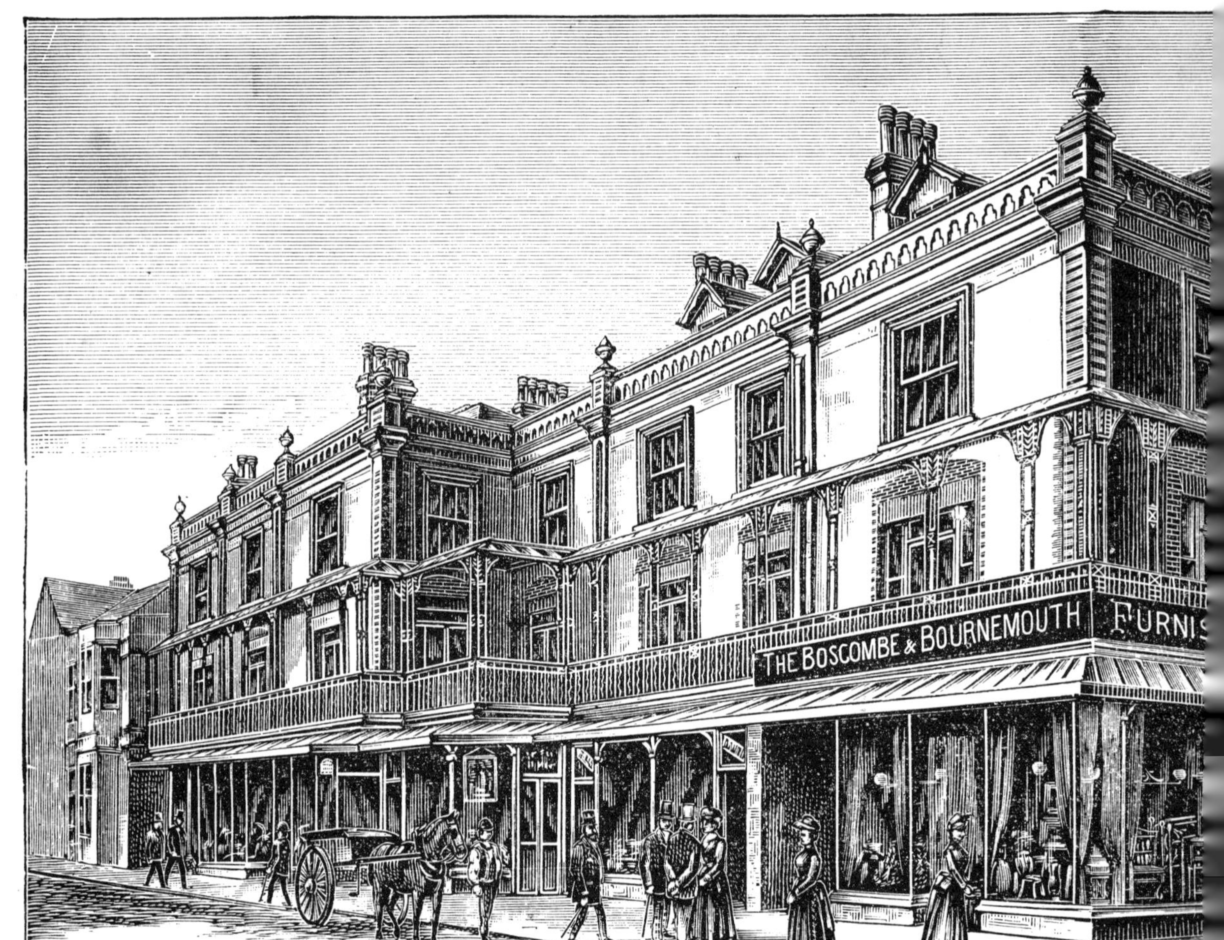

BOSCOMBE COLONNADE. BARNBY, BENDALL, & GOODM

W. H. STEWART, "THE STORES."

THE BOURNEMOUTH
AND BOSCOMBE
Pantechnicon.

J. C. NUTT, Proprietor.

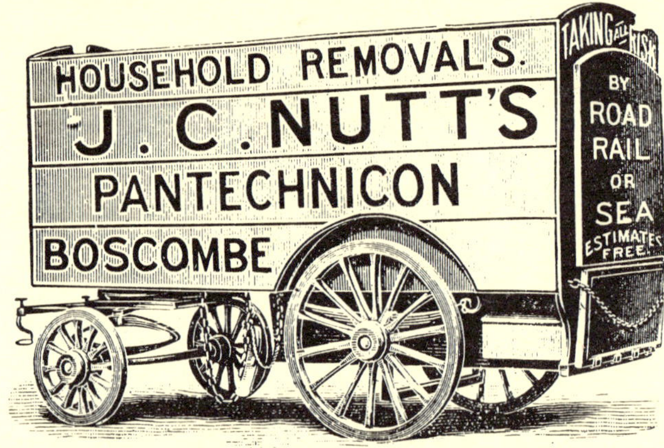

Telegrams—"NUTT, BOSCOMBE." Telephone No. 749.

Prospectuses and every information FREE on application to the Chief Office—

PALMERSTON ROAD, BOSCOMBE,

OR BRANCH OFFICE, POOLE HILL, BOURNEMOUTH.

Removing and Warehousing of Household Furniture,

Luggage, Pictures, China, Glass, Wine, Plate, Officers' Baggage, Musical Instruments, Carriages, and every description of Moveable Property,

To & from ALL PARTS of the UNITED KINGDOM & CONTINENT

In Specially-constructed Lock-up Pantechnicon Vans.

Large New Fireproof Depository for Storing purposes, which should be inspected before going elsewhere; open to view from 9.0 a.m. to 5.0 p.m.

Communications to J. C. NUTT, The Depositories,
ESTIMATES FREE. BOSCOMBE, HANTS.

Loading up. Nutt's horsedrawn pantechnicon, in about 1905.

VICTORIA
Family and Commercial Hotel,
COMMERCIAL ROAD, BOURNEMOUTH.

BAYLY'S
WINE, SPIRIT, ALE, PORTER, AND CIDER STORES.

Families supplied on the shortest notice with
EXCELLENT WINES OF CHOICE VINTAGES,
GENUINE SPIRITS,
Bass's & Allsopp's East India Pale & Burton Ales
IN CASK, BOTTLE, AND DRAUGHT
GUINNESS'S STOUT
IN CASK, BOTTLE, AND DRAUGHT,
PRIME DEVON AND SOMERSET CIDER
IN CASK, BOTTLE, AND DRAUGHT;
LIQUEURS,
Lemonade, Soda & Seltzer Waters, & Ginger Beer.

GOOD STABLING AND LOCK-UP COACH HOUSE.
NEAT PONY PHAETON.
BROUGHAMS, WAGGONETTES & SADDLE HORSES.

Belle Vue and Pier Family and Boarding Hotel,
BOURNEMOUTH,
WILLIAM MANSFIELD BILL, PROPRIETOR.

This well-known Hotel is delightfully situated close to the Sea-shore and the Pier, commanding extensive views of the English Channel, the Isles of Wight and Purbeck, &c.; it is replete with every comfort and convenience, and is visited by families of the highest station and respectability.

WINES AND SPIRITS IMPORTED.
Families supplied at their own residences with Wines and Spirits of the finest quality;
DRAUGHT & BOTTLED ALES, &c., AT WHOLESALE PRICES.

POSTING IN ALL ITS BRANCHES.
EXCELLENT STABLING WITH LOCK-UP COACH HOUSES.

HOT AND COLD BATHS CLOSE TO THE HOTEL.
A SPACIOUS BILLIARD ROOM.
ASSEMBLY ROOMS FOR BALLS, CONCERTS, &c.

N.B.—Good Pike and Perch Fishing for Visitors at this Hotel, within an asy distance.

WILLIAM COATES,
RIDING MASTER,
LANSDOWNE HOTEL STABLES,
Old Christchurch Road,
AND
ORCHARD STREET LIVERY STABLES,
Commercial Road,
BOURNEMOUTH.

SADDLE HORSES & PONIES,
SOCIABLES, PARK PHAETONS,
Broughams, Waggonettes, Croyden Baskets, &c.

A large Family Waggonette and Private Omnibus.

DONKEYS AND INVALID CHAIRS.
LADIES' HABITS.

BRANKSOME ESTATE OFFICE.

T. J. HANKINSON,
House and Estate Agent,
BOURNEMOUTH, HANTS.

AGENT TO THE ROYAL INSURANCE COMPANY FOR FIRE AND LIFE
THE ECONOMIC LIFE, THE LAW FIRE, AND THE NORWICH UNION INSURANCE OFFICES.

Families requiring Houses or Apartments are respectfully requested to apply as above.

Agent to the Architectural Pottery Company, Poole.

RICHMOND STABLES,
BOURNEMOUTH.

NEAT PONY PHEATONS, &c.

BROUGHAMS, WAGGONETTES, AND SADDLE HORSES FOR HIRE.

H. RICHARDS, (LATE W. HARRIS,) PROPRIETOR.

RIDING LESSONS.

"The Historic House."

ELECTRIC PASSENGER LIFTS.

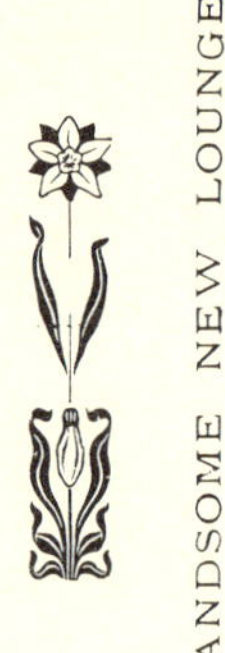

HANDSOME NEW LOUNGE.

Newlyn's Hotel.

Residence of the Founder of Bournemouth, 1810, and H.I.M. Empress of Austria, 1888.

Royal Exeter.

FIRST-CLASS.

COMMANDING FINE VIEWS OF PINE WOODS AND ISLE OF WIGHT.

PROPRIETOR: HENRY NEWLYN, J.P.

Two Minutes from the Pier. Opposite the Winter Gardens.

The Lansdowne Hotel.

For Families and Gentlemen.

Pleasantly Situated on the East Cliff, near the celebrated Pines, Sea, and Principal Railway Station.

Unsurpassed for Cleanliness, Comfort and Good Cooking.

Tariff Strictly Moderate. **Telephone No. 101.**

BILLIARDS. POSTING.

Proprietor—
W. HUMPHRY, Wine and Spirit Merchant.

STAMP OFFICE.
T. J. HANKINSON,
BOOKSELLER, STATIONER, PRINTER,
AND MUSIC SELLER,
House and Estate Agent,
Ladies' Fancy and Berlin Wool Repository,
BOURNEMOUTH.
CIRCULATING LIBRARY.
MUDIE'S NEWEST BOOKS.
ENGRAVING IN ALL ITS BRANCHES.
Newspapers and Periodicals punctually supplied.
PIANOS & HARMONIUMS FOR SALE OR HIRE.
Bagatelle and Croquet for Sale or Hire.
MAGIC LANTERN FOR HIRE.
Photographic and other Views of Bournemouth and the neighbourhoo
CUMBERLAND HOUSE,
(Facing the Telegraph Office)
BOURNEMOUTH.
W. C. ALLISON,
Hair Cutter, Ornamental Hair Manufact
and Perfumer,
Begs most respectfully to solicit the attention of the Nobility, Gentry, and Inhabitants of Bournemouth and its vicinity, to the above Establishment, where both Ladies and Gentlemen may depend on having their Hair properly Cut, Cleaned, and Dressed, the proprietor having had considerable experience in first-class houses in London, Cambridge, and Brighton.
W. C. A. has received, and gratefully acknowledges, the kind patronage already bestowed on him by most of the leading families residing in and visiting this fashionable Watering-place, and hopes by strict personal attention to merit, and receive a continuance of their support.
THE CHARGES ARE
FOR LADIES, 1s. FOR GENTLEMEN, 6d.
AT THEIR OWN RESIDENCES, 6d. EXTRA.
N.B.—Every description of Ornamental Hair or
premises, and Lessons given in every mode of Ladies'
SHAMPOOIN
On the same principle as at Douglas's,
Truefitt's, Burlingto
PROMENADE
Library and Reading Rooms,
(Close to the Pier, and adjoining the Baths)
BOURNEMOUTH,
ESTABLISHED 1840.
D., E., & A. SYDENHAM,
BOOKSELLERS,
GENERAL AND FANCY STATIONERS.
PIANO-FORTES LET ON HIRE.
GUIDE BOOKS, MAPS, AND VIEWS
OF BOURNEMOUTH AND THE NEIGHBOURHOOD.
A large collection of Photographic Views of Bournemouth.
A large Stock of Berlin Wools, Patterns, Canvas, French Embroidery Patterns, Cottons, Silks, Braids, and Materials for every description of Fancy Work.
Newest Books from Mudie's Library.
Newspapers and all Periodical Publications promptly supplied.
THE TIMES AND OTHER PAPERS LENT OUT TO READ.
Stereoscopes and Slides.
Photographic Albums, Portraits and Scraps.
A VARIETY OF CHILDREN'S TOYS.
BASKETS, CARRIAGE BAGS & CAMP STOOLS.
Agents for Huntley and Palmer's Reading Biscuits.
DENT'S BEST KID GLOVES.
SOAPS, SCENTS, AND PERFUMERY.
Soda Water, Lemonade, and Ginger Beer.
CROQUET AND BAGATELLE ON HIRE.
Note Paper, stamped with the principal Addresses in Bournemouth.
Printing and Bookbinding neatly executed.

Transport

The opportunities of intercourse with other parts of the kingdom are very complete, two coaches passing daily through the place, and other modes of conveyance being very numerous. The Emerald coach passes through for Christchurch, Lymington, Lyndhurst, Southampton and London, every day at twelve o'clock at noon; and the Emerald also, for the West, via Poole and Wareham, to Dorchester and Weymouth, passes through Bournemouth at three p.m. From Poole, coaches proceed daily to London, Bath, Bristol, and other parts, and the west of England can be reached from Dorchester or Weymouth. Facilities for visiting the Isle of Wight and the south-east coast may be found at Southampton. *First Bournemouth Guide, 1840.*

A charming donkey-cart group in one of the Chines in 1900.

The Railways - the South-Western Company from Ringwood, the main line junction, which runs through Herne and Christchurch to Bournemouth. The station is situated at the extreme east end of Bournemouth on the Holdenhurst Road. It was enlarged and improved in 1874, and has since been enlarged to meet the requirements of the place.

Bournemouth Guide, 1883.

Steamboats and steamboat Excursions - In speed, efficiency, and comfort, the Bournemouth Steamboats cannot be surpassed by those of any other sea-side town on the South Coast of England. During seven months of the year, from April to October, two rival companies run daily trips from the Pier.

Brights Guide to Bournemouth, 1890

Hackney Carriages of all kinds are abundant, and may be obtained at any of the numerous cabstands. Well-appointed coaches and chars-a-banc leave the Square daily from about Easter to November.

Bournemouth Guide, 1899

This fine picture of a pony and trap, taken around 1890 in Bournemouth woods shows the common mode of transport for those days.

This Edwardian lady takes her life in her hands as she rides with her son in a basket-work side-car.

Cycle & Motor Co.,

LIMITED,

4, Dalkeith Buildings,

Bournemouth.

FACTORS :: ::
TO THE TRADE.

Telephone, 345. *Telegrams*, 'Oriel.'

First Grade Cycles and Mail Carts for Hire.

SWIFT CYCLES

Old Machines taken in part exchange.
Tuition Free in Private School to Purchasers.
REPAIRS of all description done on the Premises by Skilled Workmen.

Cash Prices from £5 0s.
Easy Terms from £6 6s.

F. MORGAN,

BICYCLE AND TRICYCLE

MANUFACTURER,

30, THE TRIANGLE,

BOURNEMOUTH.

BICYCLES AND TRICYCLES FOR HIRE.

A Large Stock of New Machines to select from.

EASY TERMS OF PAYMENT.

TRIPS! TRIPS!! TRIPS!!!

DELIGHTFUL OUTINGS.

THE "CHAR-A-BANC,"

DURING THE SUMMER MONTHS,

Weather permitting, makes daily excursions in the neighbourhood of

BOURNEMOUTH,

INCLUDING

Corfe Castle, Bindon Abbey, New Forest, Rufus' Stone, Lymington, Lyndhurst, Lulworth, Woodbury Hill, Wimborne, Christchurch, Hordle (The Shakers' Encampment), &c., &c., &c.

These trips enable Visitors to enjoy the many beauties with which the vicinity of Bournemouth is surrounded.

The Char-a-Banc is admirably appointed and driven by an experienced whip.

Seats may be secured and places reserved for any journey at the Booking Office, the Victoria Library, the Square, where the vehicle daily starts from and returns to.

The fares are extremely moderate. Box seats are One Shilling extra.

The trips are arranged weekly and advertised in the local papers, and by bills about the town.

The Char-a-Bance may be engaged privately, for terms and all further particulars apply

H. LAIDLAW, Royal Mews,

CARRIAGE MANUFACTURER & JOB MASTER.

BOOKING OFFICE, THE VICTORIA LIBRARY.

Elliott's :

'Royal Blue' Coaches and **Chars-a-Banc**

To all Places of Interest.

ORDERS RECEIVED for

LANDAUS, WAGONETTES and CABS

To and From Station

Horses taken in at Livery.

Lessons given in Tandem or Four-in-Hand Driving,

The ROYAL BLUE COACH will make a Special Run to BARTON COURT HOTEL and BARTON CLIFFS every Thursday during the Winter Months.

Leaving the Royal Exeter Hotel (Newlyn's) at **10.40** a.m. and the Square at **10.45** a.m.

BOOKING OFFICE (where Seats can be Booked in Advance—

'Royal Blue' and Branksome Mews,

TELEPHONE No. 262.

Avenue Lane, Avenue Road, Bournemouth.

ELLIOTT'S

'Royal Blue'

Coaches : : and Chars-a-banc

Run DAILY to the NEW FOREST and other Places of Interest in the District.

Landaus, Wagonettes, and Cabs

To and from the Stations.

Horses taken in at Livery,

LESSONS given in TANDEM or FOUR-IN-HAND DRIVING.

Booking Office (where Seats can be booked in advance):

Royal Blue and Branksome Mews,

Avenue Lane, Avenue Road, Bournemouth.

Telephone No. **262.**

This splendid outing party in the Square was photographed in about 1908. With the char-a-banc's solid tyres, strong nerves and an iron constitution were needed!

The show piece of the Bournemouth Tramway fleet in 1905 in the Square. The only single deck tram in the fleet, it was officially the Mayor's car used for all official occasions and was lent out to stores to advertise sales etc. It ended its days as a bus-shelter at Iford Bridge in 1935.

The 1905 view of The Square. The tramcar is number 7 and on the right is the Hackney Carriage stand.

An Edwardian photograph of Bournemouth tramcar number 35 in Holdenhurst Road, en route to Boscombe. The fire station is on the right. Part of the original façade has been incorporated in the building which stands today.

Conversion and painting of Poole tramcar number 8, at the Southcote Road depot, on its takeover by Bournemouth Tramways in 1905.

Tramcar number 6 at the Lansdowne on its way to Boscombe about 1905.

An unusual sight - a tram leaves Boscombe for Bournemouth, while an aircraft flies overhead. The photograph was probably taken during the International Aviation Meeting in 1910.

The great tram accident of May 1st, 1908. It was the first and the largest tram accident in the United Kingdom. On a sunny Friday evening, about 7 p.m., the tram was approaching The Square from Poole. The magnetic brakes failed, causing car 72 to gain a speed of 70-75 m.p.h. (the normal speed was 8 m.p.h.) whereupon it became de-railed and crashed into the garden of Fairlight Glen. Seven passengers were killed and twenty-six injured. Driver W. Wilton, despite serious injuries, behaved most courageously and was subsequently exonerated of responsibility. He later became an inspector.

The pagoda in Avenue Road. The site of the Great Tram Disaster as it is today.

THE CHANNEL STEAMSHIP "WINDSOR CASTLE."

The Steamship "Windsor Castle."

THIS magnificent Channel Paddle Steamer is the latest addition to the fleet of the Bournemouth Steam Packet Company. So popular have the excursions to the numerous places of beauty and of historical interest which lie within easy reach of Bournemouth become, that the favourite Steamers of the Bournemouth Company were found to be quite inadequate, and the result was the courageous and far-sighted determination of the Directors to build a vessel unequalled for speed, strength, and accommodation by any on the South Coast. Such the *Windsor Castle* unquestionably is. Her dimensions are—length, 260 feet; breadth, 64 feet 6 inches over paddles; depth, 19 feet 6 inches.

Her Engines are of the Triple-Expansion Type, of 2,400 h.p. indicated, which give the vessel a speed of 17 knots per hour. The Dining Saloons, of which there are three below the main deck, are of the most modern and well-appointed description, communicating one with the other by means of water-tight Automatic Sliding Doors. There is also ample Saloon accommodation below the fore deck. A magnificent Day Saloon, superbly fitted, is provided, also a spacious First-Class Ladies' Saloon, Private Saloon, and Lavatories. The deck erections—in fact, the hull throughout—are all of steel, constructed to pass the highest test both of the Board of Trade and Lloyd's for Channel Service. Every provision has been made for perfect equipment—such as Steam Steering Gear Fore and Aft, Electric Light, and Buoyant Life-Saving Appliances. The other vessels belonging to this Company are the *Brodick Castle* and the *Lord Elgin*.

THE SALOON OF THE STEAMSHIP "WINDSOR CASTLE."

Bournemouth Queen in 1910. She joined the local fleet in 1908 and like the 'Emperor of India' served in both World Wars, returning to normal duties in the Second World War on July 19th, 1947.

SS Brodick Castle in the Bay in 1900. Following the wreck of "SS Bournemouth" in 1886, she joined the local fleet in 1887 and in 1908, suffered a similar fate off Portland, whilst en route for the Argentine for use as a cattle boat.

The view from the pier head looking towards Bournemouth in 1910.

Paddle steamers were extremely popular as pleasure boats. This Edwardian photograph shows one tied up to the pier and one approaching.

An early Edwardian photograph of Bournemouth's east beach showing the pleasure boats and the bathing machines in the background.

The "Marie Theresa" off Hengistbury Head in 1898, where it was wrecked while bound for Poole carrying a cargo of brickettes.

Bournemouth East (now the Central) Station under construction in 1884. St. Paul's Church can be seen in the background.

Bournemouth West Station photographed about 1912.

Bournemouth Central Station photographed about 1904.

Services

Bournemouth Volunteer Fire Brigade. The Brigade is now at full strength, having, besides the Officers, 3 foremen, 3 engineers, 20 firemen and 1 station fireman, the latter in the employ of the Town Council. The Brigade can be summoned from any of the numerous telephone points in the Borough, the Operators at the exchange taking the duty of calling the Brigade. Every member is in connection with the centre, either by telephone or electric bell. Horses are supplied from the nearest livery stables, and are also called by electric bells.

Bright's Guide to Bournemouth, 1896.

Bournemouth Police Station at Madeira Road built in 1869, showing Sergeant Coles and three Constables who were the entire Police Force when this photograph was taken in 1870. Those arrested and charged were marched to Christchurch to appear before the Magistrates.

The Bournemouth Police, Boscombe Sub-Division in 1903.

The Mounted Police Section was disbanded in 1922. This photograph shows the last horse and rider.

METROPOLITAN POLICE

MURDER

AND MUTILATION.

Portraits, Description and Specimen of Handwriting of HAWLEY HARVEY CRIPPEN, alias Peter Crippen, alias Franckel; and ETHEL CLARA LE NEVE, alias Mrs. Crippen, and Neave.

Wanted for the Murder of CORA CRIPPEN, otherwise Belle Elmore; Kunigunde Mackamotzki; Marsangar and Turner, on, or about, 2nd February last.

Description of Crippen. Age 50, height 5 ft. 3 or 4, complexion fresh, hair light brown, inclined sandy, scanty, bald on top, rather long scanty moustache, somewhat straggly, eyes grey, bridge of nose rather flat, false teeth, medium build, throws his feet outwards when walking. May be clean shaven or wearing a beard and gold rimmed spectacles, and may possibly assume a wig.

Sometimes wears a jacket suit, and at other times frock coat and silk hat. May be dressed in a brown jacket suit, brown hat and stand up collar (size 15).

Somewhat slovenly appearance, wears his hat rather at back of head.

Very plausible and quiet spoken, remarkably cool and collected demeanour.

Speaks French and probably German. Carries Firearms.

An American citizen, and by profession a Doctor.

Has lived in New York, Philadephia, St. Louis, Detroit, Michigan, Coldwater, and other parts of America.

May obtain a position as assistant to a doctor or eye specialist, or may practise as an eye specialist, Dentist, or open a business for the treatment of deafness, advertising freely.

Has represented Munyon's Remedies, in various cities in America.

Crippen's handwriting

39 Hilldrop Crescent
Feb 2/10

Dear Miss May
Illness of a near relative has called me to America on only a few hours notice, so I must ask you bring my resignation as treasurer before the meeting today, so that a new treasurer can be elected at once. You will appreciate my haste when I tell you I have not been to bed all night, packing and getting ready to go.

Description of Le Neve alias Neave.—A shorthand writer and typist, age 27, height 5 ft. 5, complexion pale, hair light brown (may dye same), large grey or blue eyes, good teeth, nice looking, rather long straight nose (good shape), medium build, pleasant, lady-like appearance. Quiet, subdued manner, talks quietly, looks intently when in conversation. A native of London.

Le Neve's handwriting

39. Hilldrop Cres

Dear [illegible]
Am so sorry dear to disappoint you to day have been called away. Will write you later. My love dear to you all & kisses.
From your Loving Sis
Ethel

Dresses well, but quietly, and may wear a blue serge costume (coat reaching to hips) trimmed heavy braid, about ½ inch wide, round edge, over shoulders and pockets. Three large braid buttons down front, about size of a florin, three small ones on each pocket, two on each cuff, several rows of stitching round bottom of skirt; or a light grey shadow-stripe costume, same style as above, but trimmed grey moire silk instead of braid, and two rows of silk round bottom of skirt; or a white princess robe with gold sequins; or a mole coloured striped costume with black moire silk collar; or a dark Vieuxrose cloth costume, trimmed black velvet collar; or a light heliotrope dress.

May have in her possession and endeavour to dispose of same:—a round gold brooch, with points radiating zig-zag from centre, each point about an inch long, diamond in centre, each point set brilliants, the brooch in all being slightly larger than a half-crown; and two single stone diamond rings, and a diamond and sapphire (or ruby) ring, stones rather large.

Absconded 9th inst. and may have left, or will endeavour to leave the country.

Please cause every enquiry at Shipping Offices, Hotels, and other likely places, and cause ships to be watched.

Information to be given to the Metropolitan Police Office, New Scotland Yard, London. S.W., or at any Police Station.

E. R. HENRY,
The Commissioner of Police of the Metropolis.

Metropolitan Police Office,
New Scotland Yard. *16th July, 1910.*

(17086–1) Wt. P 1367 285n 2000 7/10 D & S.

Jumpers Corner Tea Rooms near Iford, photographed after a heavy storm in the 1930's. The lady standing in the foreground is Miss Ethel le Neve, who was implicated with Dr. Crippen, the infamous wife murderer. He was executed and she was freed, having been found not guilty. For forty years, she was the proprietress of this cafe.

Ethel le Neve's cafe as it is today.

A Police outing leaving Boscombe Sub-Division on the 3rd July, 1908.

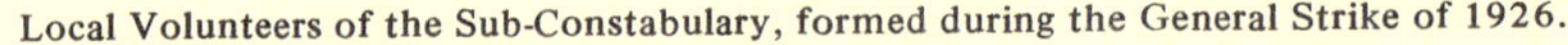

Local Volunteers of the Sub-Constabulary, formed during the General Strike of 1926.

Bournemouth East Volunteer Fire Brigade, pictured about 1913 in front of their new petrol-motor fire appliance.

Bournemouth Volunteer Fire Brigade, Holdenhurst Road in 1902, going out on call.

Bournemouth Fire Services competition winners in 1902.

The early fire service was a voluntary organisation. This 1903 photograph of the Bournemouth Volunteer Fire Brigade shows Mr. E. L. Lane, the undertaker, as captain (seated in the centre) with Alderman Robson, the grocer, and one time Mayor of Bournemouth, as second officer, seated to the right of Lane.

Horse-drawn appliance of the Bournemouth Fire Brigade pulling out of the station in Holdenhurst Road in 1902.

The same scene today with a modern Dennis appliance. The original facade of the fire station (see above) has been slightly altered and enlarged, but otherwise the building is the same.

George Fox, a remarkable eccentric. One-time licensee of the Tregonwell Arms, he was Bournemouth's first postmaster. He died in 1870.

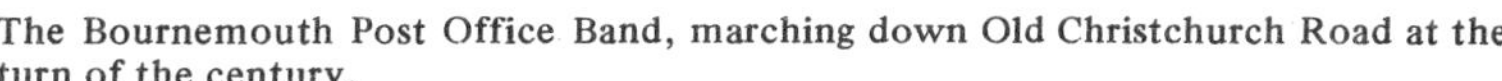

The Bournemouth Post Office Band, marching down Old Christchurch Road at the turn of the century.

Edward Green, conductor of the Bournemouth Post Office Band.

A Bournemouth postman, photographed around 1905.

A Post has been established between Bournemouth and Poole, arriving at the former place at eight a.m., and departing thence at twenty minutes before six o'clock p.m. The Post Office is at the Tregonwell's Arms Inn. For the accommodation of visitors there is a receiving box at the Library.

First Bournemouth Guide, 1840.

The Post and Money Order Office is at Mr. Bell's, grocer, Commercial Road. There are two deliveries of letters daily - the mail arrives at half-past six in the morning, and the box closes again at eight o'clock; the day mail arrives at five o'clock, and the office closes at eight in the evening.

Electric Telegraph - The station of the Poole and Bournemouth Printing Telegraph is a Mr. Rebbeck's Office, which is open daily for the transmission of messages to all parts of the kingdom, at moderate rates.

Bournemouth Guide, 1867.

Nurses and patients at "Mont Dore" when it was a military hospital during the First World War.

Royal Victoria Hospital, Bournemouth. *(Alexandra Ward.)*

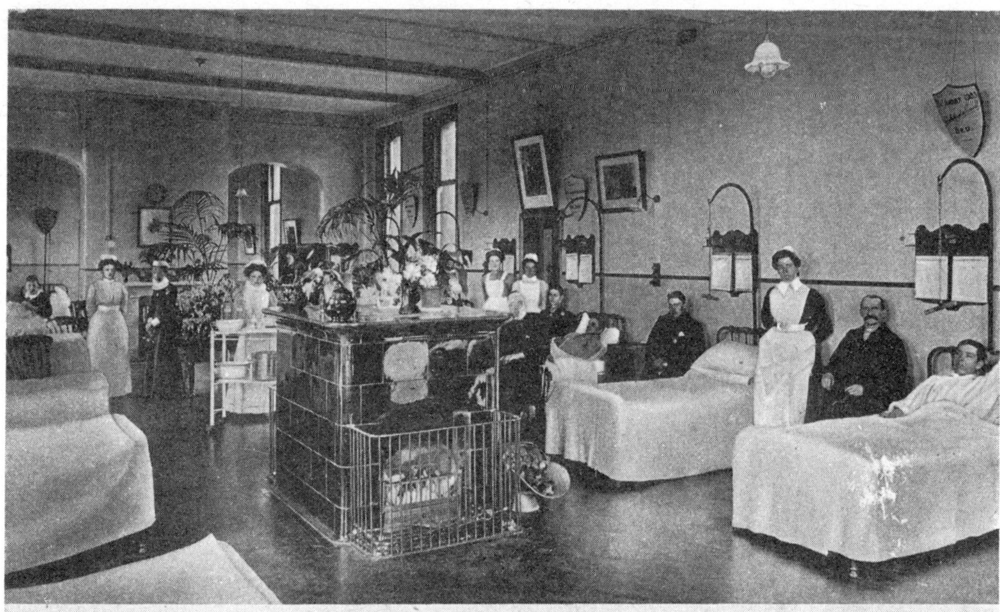

Royal Victoria Hospital, Bournemouth. *(Albert Edward Ward.)*

A Cantata,

"THE CHILDREN'S CRUSADE,"

WILL BE GIVEN BY THE SCHOLARS IN

THE BRITISH SCHOOL, BOURNEMOUTH,

ON

THURSDAY, APRIL 30TH, 1891.

DOORS OPEN AT 7.30 COMMENCE AT 8.

PROCEEDS TO BE DEVOTED TO THE PURCHASE OF A HARMONIUM.

SECOND SEATS – SIXPENCE.

Anglo-German College for Ladies.

Principal - - - *MARIA SCHOLEFIELD.*

(Geb. Macat.)

PUPILS ADMITTED FOR SHORT PERIODS TO SUIT THE CONVENIENCE OF VISITORS.

A SEPARATE CLASS for VERY YOUNG CHILDREN,

FROM FOUR TO SEVEN YEARS OF AGE,

CONDUCTED ON THE GERMAN KINDER-GARTEN SYSTEM.

Prospectuses, &c., can be obtained at Hankinson's Library.

"Scholars" of the British School in Bournemouth.

The British School, at the Lansdowne, pictured at the end of the last century.

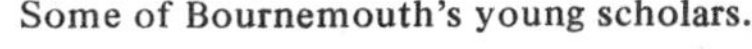

Some of Bournemouth's young scholars.

Bournemouth Square, about 1868.

Then & Now

An early line engraving showing Commercial Road as it appeared in the 19th century.

The same area photographed at the turn of the century.

Bournemouth Square photographed about 1935.

Bournemouth Square as it appears today, photographed from a similar angle.

Looking down Commercial Road in 1910.

Poole Hill 1905. At the right is my energetic mother on her bicycle.

The West Hill Post Office in 1900. Today the Post Office is on the opposite side of the road.

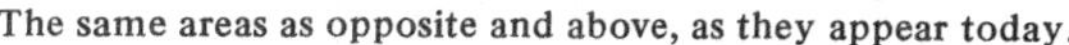
The same areas as opposite and above, as they appear today.

Middle Road, Westbourne, in 1907. The shop development in Seamore Road in the background was the successful venture of Henry Joy, the builder of Bournemouth Arcade.

The same view today. The road has been re-named Robert Louis Stevenson Avenue, after the author. He lived in "Skerryvore", a house on the seaward end of the road. He stayed in Bournemouth between 1884 and 1887, during which time he wrote "Kidnapped" and "Dr. Jekyll and Mr. Hyde".

The Queen's Hotel and West Station Approach with its waiting cabs, photographed in 1903.

The same area today. With the exception of the Hotel, all has disappeared and been replaced by the Wessex Way.

The Poole to Christchurch tram on its way through Westbourne in 1909.

Skerryvore in Westbourne, the home of Robert Louis Stevenson, which was damaged in an air raid in 1940. It was then demolished and a public garden established as a memorial.

County Gates in 1900. The Lodge of the former Branksome Towers Estate now demolished was situated at the end of the drive which is now the Avenue. Today the site forms part of the vast roundabout with office buildings.

A beach-side view of Branksome Chine.

Branksome Chine in 1928.

An Edwardian view of Branksome Chine.

Branksome Chine today.

Once the home of Aubrey Beardsley, controversial illustrator of the "Yellow Book" and leading exponent of Art Nouveau, this building, then called "Muriel" and not "Murial" as in the line engraving above, was built by Joseph Cutler. It still stands at the junction of Terrace Road and Exeter Road.

'Muriel' as it appears today. Inset is an example of Beardsley's book illustration.

The Square, looking towards Old Christchurch Road in 1899.

Looking up Old Christchurch Road today, some of the original buildings remain on the left, but the buildings on the right have been re-built.

EMPRESS HOTEL
THE EMPRESS HOTEL
NATIONAL PROVINCIAL
POOLE
BOURNEMOUTH CORPORATION TRAMWAYS

The arrow points to the premises of Riddett and Ede, Estate Agents, now Riddett and Adams Smith, situated on Richmond Hill. W. H. Smith and Son Ltd. still occupies the same premises. The photograph was taken some time in the 1920's.

Plummer Roddis Ltd., the department store in Old Christchurch Road. This photograph, taken in 1920, also shows Brights (now Dingles).

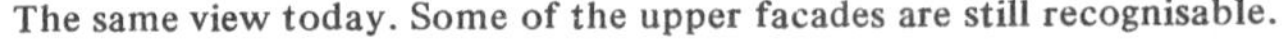

The same view today. Some of the upper facades are still recognisable.

Plummer Roddis and Tyrrell's store (now Roddis House) in Old Christchurch Road, dressed for the occasion of the accession of King Edward VII in 1901.

Looking down Old Christchurch Road past Brights and towards Plummers. The decorations are for the Bournemouth Fetes of 1910.

Looking down Old Christchurch Road today.

The corner of Hinton Road in 1895. The entrance to St. Peter's is on the right, and Old Christchurch Road is in the distance.

The same view today. Beales department store now occupies the whole of the left corner. Dingles, (previously Allen's) occupies the other corner.

In 1908, A. H. Butt, the Art dealer, had his shop where Beales Book shop stands today.

Beales, Gervis Place corner today.

An early line engraving of St. Peter's Church without a spire.

St. Peter's Church in 1879, photographed soon after completion of the spire, which was added in that year. Church House, the site of the present Beales department store is on the left.

St. Peter's School Room in 1910 which occupied the present site of Maples from 1852 to 1937.

Maples Department Store in St. Peter's Road today. Built in 1937 on the site of St. Peters School.

Gervis Place entrance to the Arcade in 1878. The building on the left was the town's Post Office from 1875 to 1883. Note the wrought iron gates of the Arcade.

Gervis Place junction with Westover Road today. Austin Reed and Dingles flower shop with the Arcade and the modern Beales in the background, are a familiar sight.

A 1912 view of the band playing in the outside Tea Gardens of the Westover Palace. It was a popular rendezvous of those days.

Westover Road today.

A view down Richmond Hill in 1880. A milkman making his way down the hill on his cart.

Richmond Hill, from the same view-point today. By coincidence, a modern milkfloat is in the same position.

Looking down Richmond Hill in 1910.

Bristol and West House on the corner of Post Office Road and Richmond Hill. It was built on the site of the Punshon Memorial Church (seen in the 1890 photograph on the right) which was destroyed by bombing in 1943.

"The Tantivy" in 1910. A jolly coach party outside the "Cri" in Old Christchurch Road. The entrance to the first Town Hall buildings is on the left.

The picture today in Old Christchurch Road, now partly a pedestrian way except for public transport. The entrance to the Criterion Arcade is on the left, formerly the first Town Hall.

Holy Trinity Church in Old Christchurch Road, in 1906. Built in 1867-69, its imposing tower was added in 1878. "Cren Dahr", the house on the left, is now the local Registrar's Offices.

The same view today.

The view from the pier by Exeter Road in 1920. The horse trough in the centre foreground is now at Horse-Shoe Common. The superb open cars in the taxi rank would be much sought-after as collector's items today.

The same view today.

The Belle Vue and Pier Hotel in 1880 opened in 1839. Almost a "Wild-West" scene with its posting and livery stables.

The Pier Approach in 1860 with the materials for the pier, then under construction. The original Baths can be seen on the right and the Belle Vue Hotel.

The view of the Pier Approach in 1934. Sydenham's Baths and Reading Rooms were demolished the following year and the skeleton of the Palace Court Hotel rises in the background.

The ever-so-slightly changing face of the pleasure gardens. Children's corner at the beginning of the century.

Children's corner in 1920.

Top: The Invalid's Walk (now Pine Walk) in 1906.

Left: Children's corner just before the First World War.

Children's corner today.

A view of Boscombe Hill in 1910.

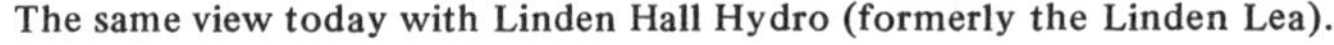

The same view today with Linden Hall Hydro (formerly the Linden Lea).

A typical Edwardian scene. Listening to the band in the Crescent Gardens, Boscombe.

Crescent Gardens today. The sound of music has been replaced by the sound of traffic.

Sea Road, Boscombe, in 1905, looking towards Christchurch Road and the entrance to the Royal Arcade.

Sea Road today.

ɔ: Christchurch Road, Boscombe, in 1901. A iceman stands outside the entrance to the Royal :ade, which was opened by the Duke of ınaught on 19th December, 1893.

ht and Below: Two views of the interior of the yal Arcade, Boscombe, as it appeared at the ı of the century.

The construction of Windsor Road in the Boscombe Spa Estate in 1892. Workmen are cutting down the great pine forests which were planted 80 years earlier.

Windsor Road today.

Looking up Sea Road from Boscombe Pier. This Edwardian photograph shows one of the little donkey carts.

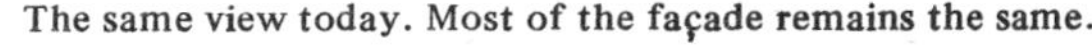

The same view today. Most of the façade remains the same.

Southbourne Pier in 1894. The pier, designed by Archibald Smith, was built by the Southbourne Pier Company in 1888. It was badly damaged by gales in December 1900, and dismantled as a dangerous structure, in 1907.

Boscombe Pier Approach in 1888.

Boscombe Pier Approach in 1909.

Boscombe Pier Approach as it is today. The middle of the pier was blown up in 1940 for anti-invasion reasons, and the approach much altered when it was eventually re-built.

Boscombe Pier and Undercliff Drive in 1913.

The same view today.

The whale which was washed ashore at Boscombe on 7th January, 1897. The skeleton was mounted on Boscombe Pier for many years and the bones were eventually ground up for fertiliser at Powell's Yard in Springbourne. Until decomposition set in, children used it as a slide.

In 1896, this was the quiet village of Iford, with Water Lane and the old bridge, which had existed as the crossing point of the Stour for hundreds of years.

The same area as it appears today.

At the turn of the century, a traction engine pulling decorated carriages over Iford Bridge.

The Old Iford Bridge which was closed to vehicular traffic in 1935, when the new bridge came into use. Before the new bridge was built, a further two arches were added to the old bridge. This photograph shows the bridge before it was enlarged.